our
Nicole
from
CZECH
part
of
the
great
EAMIE
team

Thank you for all your
support of our team!
Petra H.

Julia

Kateřina V.

Katarína

Erik

ABOUT THIS BOOK

In Prague, she "would rather be able to paint than to write", said the Romantic novelist Caroline de la Motte Fouqué, adding: "There is a point at this height from where the gaze drops away, as if drugged, into this great abundance of riches. Immediately underneath, the embankments of the Vltava, above it the royal city of Prague!" This city is indescribable, "perhaps even incomparable" – and most likely, what has fascinated visitors at all times is the fact that

"Golden Prague" – its historic heart a protected UNESCO World Heritage site – continued to change through the course of its history, yet has always remained constant – and unique. And if today, more than two decades after the "Velvet Revolution", everything continues to be in upheaval, the words of the poet Detlev von Liliencron still hold true: "All of Praha is a golden network of poems." It is for good reason that Prague was chosen as the "Prague –

Mother of all Cities" ("Praga mater urbium"), a city so rich in history and histories, in art and culture, in architectural sights and the evidence of a lively and vibrant modern metropolis right at the heart of Europe. If we follow this city's poetry, then we will realize that most of the descriptions and nicknames are often soon transformed into declarations of love. Perhaps one of the most beautiful of these epithets was coined by a Praguer, the award-winning author

Lenka Reinerová, who was born there in 1916 and died there in 2008. "Prague", she wrote, "the feminine word Praha in the Czech language", could be moody like a woman. At times the city would wear an overabundantly applied and inappropriate make-up, which however was only a superficial cover. The true visage of her home town would acquiesce to such transformations, and remain "what it always has been: our wonderfully foolish Prague".

Detail on the façade of the Rudolfinum. Built between 1875 and 1885 to the plans of Josef Zítek and Josef Schulz, the neo-Renaissance building was financed by a donation from the Bohemian Savings Bank on the occasion of its 50th anniversary. Dedicated to the arts, it is today the home of the Czech Philharmonic.

CONTENTS

"I love going for a walk through Prague at night: it is as if I could capture every sigh of its soul." (Jiří Karásek)

Photo above: The golden city is spread out on both banks of the Vltava River.
Previous pages:
1 The Astronomical Clock on the Old Town Hall
2/3 View from the Old Town bridge tower across the river, toward Prague Castle
4/5 The Smetana Museum, situated on the quay named after him (far left in the picture), commemorates the composer, Bedřich Smetana.
6/7 The Old Town Square with the Astronomical Clock on the Town Hall (left in the picture) and the two towers of the Týn Church (middle of picture)
8/9 Wenceslas Square, with the main building of the National Museum
10/11 The library at the Strahov Monastery

CONTENTS

HRADČANY

According to legend, Libuše, the legendary ancestral mother of the Bohemian Přemyslid dynasty, once looked from a hillside on the west bank of the Vltava to a rock on the opposite bank and predicted the construction of a powerful castle (Czech "hrad"), at whose feet a mighty city would one day establish itself. Her prophecy was fulfilled. Construction of the castle commenced in the ninth century, and later four settlements came into existence on the flatlands in front of it; the settlements were merged in 1784. The nucleus of the city of Prague, however, was the castle which Libuše saw in her vision.

View of Charles Bridge and Prague's Castle Hill, which has inspired the imagination of poets since time immemorial: "Nothing is better than sitting on the stone railings, shutting your eyes and allowing yourself to fly away, whoo, … right into heaven" (Egon Erwin Kisch).

PRAGUE CASTLE (PRAŽSKÝ HRAD)

PRAGUE CASTLE (PRAŽSKÝ HRAD)

The castle, situated atop the Prague hill known as "Hradčany", has dominated the city for more than a thousand years, and not only visually – the political might of the country is still based here today. Kings and emperors from the Přemyslid dynasty, as well as from the houses of Luxembourg and Habsburg, resided in the castle, and so did the communist heads of state. Today it is the official residence of the president of the Czech Republic. Duke Bořivoj I had the first earth walls and wooden palisades built here (in about 852/855 and 888/889), and the complex was added to and enlarged by many later generations of rulers. Thus Prague Castle became the largest enclosed castle complex in the world, comprising not only palaces and fortified towers but also monasteries and churches, such as the mighty St Vitus Cathedral. Altogether, the castle extends over an area of around 45 hectares (108 acres).

PRAGUE CASTLE (PRAŽSKÝ HRAD)

"Old city with towers (high above the river) ...
At its most beautiful on summer days, but
most spectacular in winter. The mists rise from
the dark river; the river which is melancholical,
yet at the same time shining; the mist steams
upward, blows up to the castle city, which rises
beyond the water, its gray, green turrets jutting
into the clouds" (Alfred Kerr).

PRAGUE CASTLE (PRAŽSKÝ HRAD)

The castle complex in its entirety forms a rare example of historical continuity. In the days of the Přemyslids, the first ruling dynasty, its fortifications in the center marked the area for all future residences. The medieval moat, however, which for centuries guarded access to the castle, has long since been filled in. Today, a wrought-iron gate stands at the entrance to the first castle courtyard, which was transformed into a court of honor around the middle of the 18th century by Nicolò Pacassi, Empress Maria Theresa's supreme court architect. The second castle courtyard is entered via a triumphal arch, named Matthias Gate after its builder, Emperor Matthias (1557–1619); through this gate, it is said, "the baroque style arrived in Bohemia". The heart of the complex is the third castle courtyard, which comprises the St Vitus Cathedral and the Old Royal Palace.

Wrestling giants by Ignaz Franz Platzer flank the entrance to Prague Castle (below; left, the changing of the castle guard, which takes place every hour). Characteristic for the complex is the fact that grand sacred buildings (far left, the equestrian statue of St George in front of St Vitus Cathedral) stand side by side with the magnificent palaces of the rulers and the small guardsmen's houses in Golden Lane.

PRAGUE CASTLE: ST VITUS CATHEDRAL (CHRÁM SVATÉHO VÍTA)

St Vitus Cathedral is the third church built in the same spot inside Prague Castle. As early as the 10th century, Duke Wenceslas (Czech Václav) of Bohemia, who was later sanctified, had a stone rotunda built here to house the arm reliquary of Vitus, an early Christian martyr. The rotunda was replaced by a three-aisled Romanesque basilica, construction of which was begun in 1061 (the laying of the foundation stone) under Duke Spytihněv II.

The foundation stone for the considerably larger gothic cathedral was laid by Charles IV, then still heir to the throne, on November 21, 1344, the date when Prague – a a bishopric since 973 – officially became an archbishopric. The main attraction on the south side of the choir is the "porta aurea", the "Golden Gate" ("zlatá braná"). Built as early as the 14th century, it was the gate through which the kings arrived for the coronation ceremonies.

PRAGUE CASTLE: ST VITUS CATHEDRAL (CHRÁM SVATÉHO VÍTA)

Left the main tower on the southern façade, oriented toward the Royal Palace and the city; below, details on the façade, as well as the glass mosaic, covering 80 sq m (861 sq ft). Created by Venetian masters, the "Golden Gate" was so named after its golden background. The mosaic is a representation of the Last Judgment, which also shows Charles IV, kneeling in prayer.

PRAGUE CASTLE: ST VITUS CATHEDRAL (CHRÁM SVATÉHO VÍTA)

Measuring 124 m (407 ft) long on the outside, 60 m (197 ft) wide in the transept, and attaining a height of around 33 m (108 ft) in the central aisle, St Vitus Cathedral is not only the largest and most important sacred building in the city but also one of the most impressive gothic cathedrals in Europe. Planning and construction was initially in the hands of the French architect Matthias of Arras (1290–1352), but it was his German successor, Peter Parler (1330/1333–1399), who was responsible for the elevated status of the church as a "key building of the 14th century" (Norbert Nußbaum). Parler significantly altered the original plans as regards the building's structural shape, floor plan and cubic capacity. The cathedral's present appearance is the result of a construction history of nearly 600 years. The final part to be completed was the neogothic western façade, with its three bronze portals.

PRAGUE CASTLE: ST VITUS CATHEDRAL (CHRÁM SVATÉHO VÍTA)

The cathedral was built as a three-aisled church with transept, choir ambulatory and a wreath of chapels at the inner choir, following the French model (below, the nave). The silver altar holding the reliquaries of St Nepomuk in the southern choir perambulatory (left) was created by the Viennese goldsmith Johann Joseph Würth in the years 1733 to 1736 to plans by Joseph Emanuel Fischer von Erlach.

PRAGUE CASTLE: ST VITUS CATHEDRAL (CHRÁM SVATÉHO VÍTA)

Reformation, Counter-Reformation and the Thirty Years' War delayed completion of the church, which remained a permanent building site for centuries. In 1842, the pillars of the nave, designed as a monumental three-aisled hall but still jutting into the sky, had to make way for neogothic alterations. A vast hole also gaped above the glass mosaic on the "Golden Gate" until well into the 19th century when a large window was added. It was not until the spirit of European romanticism had taken root that new work was planned for the cathedral. In 1844, the plans were presented by a group around Canon Václav Michal Pešina, which from 1859 was known as the St Vitus Cathedral Construction Association. Work was begun in 1861, and on September 28, 1929, the 1000th anniversary of the death of Saint Wenceslas, the three western portals were finished, marking the completion of the cathedral.

Famous contemporary artists supplied the designs for the cathedral's stained-glass windows. A particular gem is the "National Patron Saints' Window" (below right) in the New Archiepiscopal Chapel, which was built as late as the 20th century. Alphonse Mucha drew the designs for it, depicting scenes from the lives of the "Apostles of the Slavs", Saints Cyril and Methodius, in bright and shiny hues.

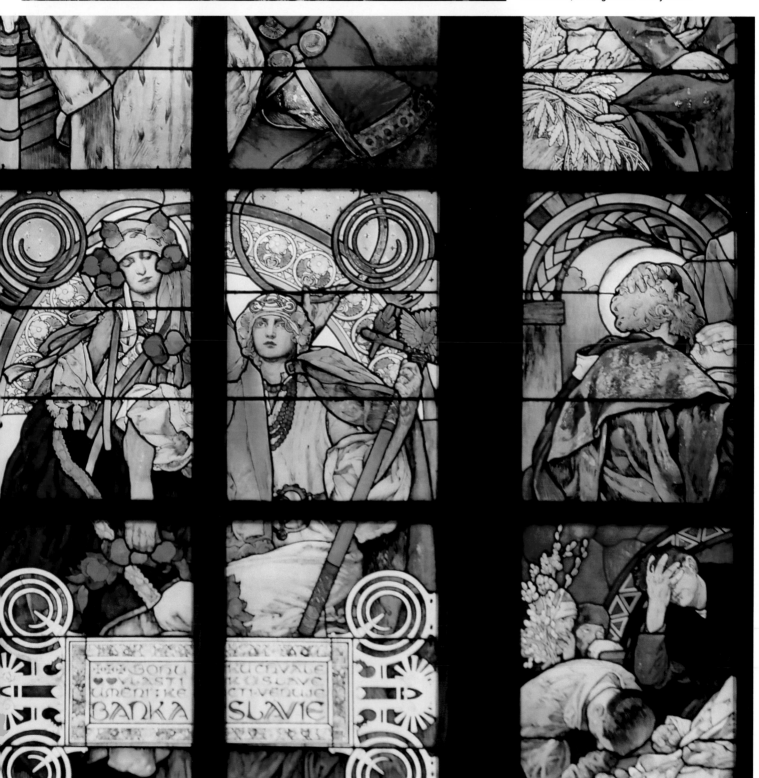

PRAGUE CASTLE: ST VITUS CATHEDRAL (CHRÁM SVATÉHO VÍTA)

The church's whole structure symbolizes the emperors' claim to the throne. It is likely that Charles IV was involved in its design. He was also instrumental in the design of the St Wenceslas Chapel, built on a square plan, contrasting on the outside and forming a sort of "structure within a structure". The chapel, faced with precious stones and gilded stucco inside, was built by Peter Parler between 1358 and 1365, in the place where a stone rotunda had previously stood. The latter had been built on the orders of St Wenceslas, and the saint was also buried here. For Charles, Wenceslas was not only an early Christian martyr but also the founder of the Bohemian state. By stylizing himself as the saint's successor (and his dynasty as the successors of the Přemyslids), Charles embued his claim to power with important symbols and signs: with a "sacred mission" and historical continuity.

PRAGUE CASTLE: ST VITUS CATHEDRAL (CHRÁM SVATÉHO VÍTA)

The St Wenceslas Chapel was to be appointed "as preciously as cannot be found anywhere else in the world". The most significant work of art is probably the statue of the saint, carved in sandstone in c. 1373 by Jindrich Parler, a nephew of the architect, and standing above the altar (below). The floor above the chapel houses the coronation chamber with the Bohemian crown jewels (left/far left, crown and imperial apple).

"SAINT WENCESLAS, DUKE OF THE CZECH LAND"

The mythical early history of the city of Prague tells the legend of Libuše, who was not only a gifted visionary but also on the lookout for a strong husband, in order to bear him strutting heirs. Her choice is said to have fallen on the farmer Přemysl, after whom the dynasty was named that would reign for several centuries. The first historically proven member of the dynasty, Duke Bořivoj (d. c. 894), moved the seat of the ruling family to the Hradčany.

In 874, he and his wife Ludmilla were christened by the Slav Apostle Methodius. His widow was murdered during the course of family disputes after his death, and in 921, one of her grandsons came to power: Duke Wenceslas (c. 903–929/935), who was described as pious, benevolent and wise. The "Good King" Wenceslas worked for both the unification and the Christianization of the country, but he was eventually murdered by his brother Boleslav, for

reasons that are still unknown. Wenceslas was proclaimed a saint in the tenth century and soon a cult developed around him. His tomb in Prague Castle became a pilgrims' destination. Veneration of St Wenceslas as a martyr and the historic founding father of the country is expressed in the Czech hymn, "Svatý Václave, vévodo české země" ("Saint Wenceslas, Duke of the Czech Land") – which was for a long time the unofficial national anthem.

"SAINT WENCESLAS, DUKE OF THE CZECH LAND"

Wenceslas is said to have continued performing his miracles even after his bones had been transferred to the St Wenceslas Chapel. In the year 2000, the saint's name day on September 28 was made an official public holiday in the Czech Republic. The painting left depicts the saint in Karlštejn Castle; below, from the left, the saint in a medieval miniature, on a historic banner and on horseback in Wenceslas Square.

PRAGUE CASTLE: OLD ROYAL PALACE (STARY KRÁLOVSKÝ PALÁC)

The three-storey Old Royal Palace served as a residence for successive rulers from the early 12th century to the second half of the 16th century. Its showpiece is the Vladislav Hall, built in the years 1493 to 1503 by Benedikt Ried, the royal architect born in the Austrian town of Piesting, on the orders of King Vladislav II. Thanks to its enormous size – length 62 m (203 ft), width 16 m (52 ft), height 13 m (43 ft) – the hall was able to accommodate markets as well as equestrian displays and tournaments. It is famed for its "Riders' Staircase" whose shallow steps made it possible for horses to access the hall. The pillarless vault is held up only by delicate ribbed vaults jutting far into the interior of the hall. On the eastern side of the hall, a passage leads to the Chapel of All Saints, originally Romanesque in style, but converted as a gothic chapel in the year 1370 by Peter Parler.

The Vladislav Hall (below left and top of picture band; underneath, the Old Diet Chamber of the Imperial Court Council and the Bohemian Chancellery) was once the venue for coronation ceremonies. Today, the presidents of the Czech Republic are sworn in here. The first floor of the Royal Palace houses the "New State Boards Chancellery", which is festooned with banners (left; far left, the All Saints Chapel).

PRAGUE CASTLE: ST GEORGE'S BASILICA (BAZILIKA SVATÉHO JIŘÍ)

On first seeing the baroque façade, which was only added in 1670, it is hard to believe that the twin-towered St George's Basilica on the north side of George's Square is the oldest preserved church within the Prague Castle complex. However, once you step through the portal, a three-aisled structure opens up whose originally Romanesque style has largely been restored during renovations. The church was dedicated in around 920 by Count Vratislav I, father of St Wenceslas, and was probably intended as a burial church for the Přemyslids. Adjoining on the basilica's north side is the Benedictine St George's Convent, which houses an outpost of the National Gallery. It was founded when Prague was raised to the status of a bishopric (973) by Duke Boleslav II, known as the Pious, and his sister Mlada, who became the first abbess of the convent, which was eventually dissolved in 1782.

Behind the baroque façade (left) of St George's Basilica, the most important Romanesque church in the city stands almost hidden from view. Below left, the interior of the three-aisled flat-roof basilica, with its raised choir square and three semicircular apsids; below right, the entrance to the pillared crypt which also boasts three aisles and is almost square. It houses a valuable stone triptych (c. 1220).

PRAGUE CASTLE: GOLDEN LANE (ZLATÁ ULIČKA)

According to legend, Emperor Rudolf II (1552 to 1612), who entertained a large entourage at court and was permanently in financial difficulties, is said to have set up alchemists' laboratories in the eleven tiny, brightly painted houses, standing in the narrow lane parallel to the city fortifications. There, lead was supposed to be transformed into gold, which is why the alleyway is also know as "goldmakers'" or "alchemists'" lane. Such experiments did actually take place at the time – the requisite laboratories, however, were housed in the Mihulka Tower, where the alchemists also lived. The small houses in Golden Lane, which had been built into the arches of the town walls in around 1540, initially served as homes for the castle guards. Later, artisans and poor people moved there. Franz Kafka rented a study at No. 22 for a while. Golden Lane was most recently completely restored in 2010/2011.

PRAGUE CASTLE: GOLDEN LANE (ZLATÁ ULIČKA)

In his novel "The Golem", Gustav Meyrink describes a house in "Golden Lane" (below left; below right, a music shop), which could only be seen by children born on a Sunday, and even then only when it was misty. Near the last house on the east side stands the defensive tower built by Benedikt Ried in 1496 (left), which also served as a prison and was named after its first inmate, the nobleman Dalibor of Kozojedy.

CLASSIC OF LITERARY MODERNISM: FRANZ KAFKA

"You could often see Kafka wandering on his own, in the streets, or in the gardens of Prague. He did not change in the slightest, if you were to join him. He liked to avoid speaking but was, if you were to talk, all ears ... He was the friend of many people, although he only permitted very few of them to become his friends" (Rudolf Fuchs). By the time Franz Kafka (1883–1924) died of tuberculosis, only a few friends and literary figures knew that the law graduate, who in his home town had been employed by an insurance company, was a passionate devotee of literature in his spare time. Only a handful of his texts had been published by then, mostly short narratives, which often had a disquieting or even disturbing effect, such as "The Metamorphosis", in which, over night, a traveling salesman turns into a giant insect. Kafka had asked his friend Max Brod (1884–1968) to destroy after his death all his manuscripts "unread". However, Brod did not stick to the agreement but began to prepare all the works for publication, thus ensuring the author's post-humous world fame. Kafka, "whose work seemed to capture the original existential spirit of humankind in the 20th century, characterized by anxiety and unrest, in a unique way" (Michael Müller), advanced to the elevated rank of "the" classic of literary modernism.

"... I carry up my evening meal and usually stay up there until midnight", Kafka said to his fiancée of many years, Felice Bauer, about his occasional poets' retreat at No. 22 Golden Lane (below). Today, the author is still omnipresent in his home town – mostly in the shape of his tremendous literary contribution, but also marketed in souvenir form (left, a jigsaw puzzle, illustrating "Kafka in Prague").

PRAGUE CASTLE: BELVEDERE PALACE (KRÁLOVSKÝ LETOHRÁDEK)

Virtually the entire Hradčany is surrounded by parklike green spaces, including the Paradise Garden, the Garden on the Ramparts and the Garden on the Bastion. From the north-western corner of the castle, one passes through Stag Moat, where once red deer were bred for the royal hunts, into the Royal Garden, which was laid out in 1534 according to the designs of Giovanni Spatio by the gardener Francesco. Ferdinand I (1503–1564), the first Habsburg ruler on the Bohemian throne, had a pleasure palace built here for his wife, Anna of Bohemia and Hungary (1503–1547), from 1538, which is also known as Belvedere ("beautiful views"). The structure, based on the model of the Orphanage (Ospedale degli Innocenti) in Florence, built more than 100 years before by Brunelleschi, is considered one of the most outstanding examples of the Italian Renaissance north of the Alps.

PRAGUE CASTLE: BELVEDERE PALACE (KRÁLOVSKÝ´ LETOHRÁDEK)

The "Singing Fountain" (below right), created – first and foremost – by the Bohemian metal founder Tomáš Jaroš on the west side of the Royal Gardens, is so named for the sound the water makes when it hits the bronze basin. The plans for the palace (left) were devised by Paolo della Stella; the complex was completed after his death in 1552 by Hans Tirol and Bonifaz Wolmut (below left, the large Ball Game House).

HRADČANY SQUARE (HRADČANSKÉ NÁMĚSTÍ)

"Hradčany" is not only the name of the hill on which stands Prague Castle, but also that of the suburb adjoining the castle in the west. Founded in around 1320 during the reign of John of Luxembourg on the orders of the burgraves of Prague, it initially consisted of not much more than present-day Hradčany Square, but during the reign of Charles IV the suburb was enlarged and surrounded by a ring of fortifications. At one time, the coronation route of the Bohemian kings went via Hradčany Square; in 1547, it was here that the leaders of the failed uprising of the Estates against Ferdinand I were executed. After the great fire of 1541, which had destroyed much of the Lesser Town and spread as far as the Castle District, all citizens' houses on Hradčany Square had to make room for new homes and palaces built for aristocrats and clerics, initially in the Renaissance, later in the baroque style.

"The square in front of Prague's royal palace looks rather elegant, despite the impoverished avenue that crosses it. This is because it is entirely surrounded by palaces" (Rainer Maria Rilke). The most beautiful is the Archiepiscopal palace on the north side of the square (below; left, a detail), about which Rilke also said it would stand "in a slightly pompous pose ... above the small homes of the prelates and canons".

HRADČANY SQUARE (HRADČANSKÉ NÁMĚSTÍ)

The south side of the square is dominated by the mighty Schwarzenberg Palace (Schwarzenberský palác), which was built between 1545 and 1563 on the orders of Count Jan Lobkowicz and later came into the Schwarzenberg Family's possession via a marriage. The architect of the three-winged complex was Augustin Vlach (Agostino Galli), an Italian, who had the façade decorated in the manner of the sgraffito: this involves scratching lines or shapes into a thin covering layer of mortar so that the underlying mortar, usually differently colored, becomes visible. While the Schwarzenberg Palace houses an outpost of the National Gallery, the similarly grand Tuscany Palace (Toskánÿ palác) on the narrow west side of the square, now serves as the Czech Republic's Ministry of Foreign Affairs. It had been the property of the Habsburg Grand Dukes of Tuscany since 1718 – hence the name.

On Hradčany Square, the past blows around
you "from the greenish darkness of the extensive
gardens with their dense foliage. It envelops you
in the semi-darkness of a portal,
in the vestibule of a palace" (Jiří Kařásek).
Below, the Schwarzenberg Palace with the
Marian Column, erected in 1726 by Ferdinand
Maximilian Brokof (on the right in the picture);
left, the façade of the Tuscany Palace.

COLLECTIONS OF THE NATIONAL GALLERY ON THE HRADČANY

The Prague National Gallery (Národní galerie v Praze) would more accurately be called the "Czech National Gallery based in Prague". It owes its existence to the "Association of Patriotic Friends of the Arts", comprising mostly Bohemian nobility and wealthy citizens. Established in the year 1796, it founded an art gallery whose collection continued to grow over time. Opened to the public since 1804, the Prague gallery is the second-oldest in Europe (after the Louvre in Paris, which opened as a museum in 1793). It was considerably enlarged in 1902 by a donation from Emperor Franz Joseph I and came into the ownership of the state in 1918 as a "national gallery". Today, the gallery's collections are distributed over several buildings in the city. On the Hradčany, in the St George's Convent, works of art from the 19th century are exhibited, with a main focus on Czech painters and sculptors. Two further collections can be visited on Hradčany Square: older European works, ranging from Antiquity to the Baroque, are exhibited at the Sternberg Palace, while those pieces that can be classified as Bohemian baroque are housed at the Schwarzenberg Palace. Altogether, the National Gallery's collections comprise some 14,000 paintings, 7,600 sculptures, 243,000 graphic works, 61,000 drawings and 12,000 examples of Oriental art.

A particularly valuable painting owned by the National Gallery, not only in financial terms, is Albrecht Dürer's "Feast of Rose Garlands" (below; left the art collection in Schwarzenberg Palace) of 1506, held by the Sternberg Palace. Dürer immortalized himself on the right in the painting, a piece of paper in his hand naming him as the creator of this altar picture, painted for the San Bartolomeo Church in Venice.

LORETO SANCTUARY (LORETA)

This pilgrimage center testifies to the veneration of the Virgin Mary, which experienced a heyday in 1620, after the Catholic victory in the Battle of White Mountain in Bohemia, for it was believed that the "orthodox Christians" were victorious against the Protestants thanks to the intervention of the Mother of Jesus. The Marian sanctuary on the Hradčany was founded in the year 1626 by Countess Benigna Katharina of Lobkowicz, under the supervision from the monks of the nearby Capucin monastery. The architect Giovanni Battista Orsi, a native of Como, was commissioned with its construction. The spiritual heart of the complex, completed in 1631, is the Santa Casa – a copy of the "original" in the pilgrimage village of Loreto near Ancona. According to legend, the Virgin Mary had lived there for four years, before it was brought to Italy in 1294 by four angels, in order to protect it from nonbelievers.

The Santa Casa (left) is hidden in the interior courtyard of a baroque square of buildings. It stands in the middle of the cloister, completed in 1634, three years after this copy had been built, and raised by a further floor in 1740. Christoph Dientzenhofer and his son Kilian Ignaz designed a unified front façade for the pilgrimage site on Loreto Square (Loretánské náměsti), which was built from 1721 (below).

REFORMATION AND WARS OF RELIGION

Even before Martin Luther, movements striving for a reformation of the Church existed in Bohemia. The impetus came from Jan Hus (c. 1369–1415), a theologian – and for a while also the director of the Charles University –, who under the influence of the English theologian and clerical reformer John Wycliffe (1320–1348) denounced the good life enjoyed by the clerics. He also lashed out in his sermons, held in the Czech language, against the sale of indulgences and railed against the Church's hierarchical structures. In response he was burned by the Council of Constance, which in the eyes of his followers made him a martyr. Four years later, in 1419, the "First Defenestration" took place in the New Town Hall, igniting the "Hussite Wars". This was also a conflict between ethnic groups, with the reforming Czechs fighting for equality with the upper classes, the "German Bohemians". Almost exactly 200 years later, when Bohemia was under the rule of the Catholic Habsburg dynasty, a large part of the country's nobility was Protestant. When Matthias I curtailed religious freedoms to an ever greater degree, some of the aristocrats threw three Catholic officials out of the window of the Bohemian Chancellery. This "Second Defenestration of Prague" (1618) precipitated both the Bohemian Revolt and the Thirty Years' War.

The "Second Prague Defenestration" on
May 23, 1618 (below a photogravure dating from
1889 and based on a painting by Wenceslas of
Brozik), is considered to have triggered the
Thirty Years' War (1618 to 1648). Famous in this
context was the Battle of White Mountain (near
Prague), where the troops of the Catholic League
inflicted a devastating defeat on the rebels (left
a paining by Pieter Snayers).

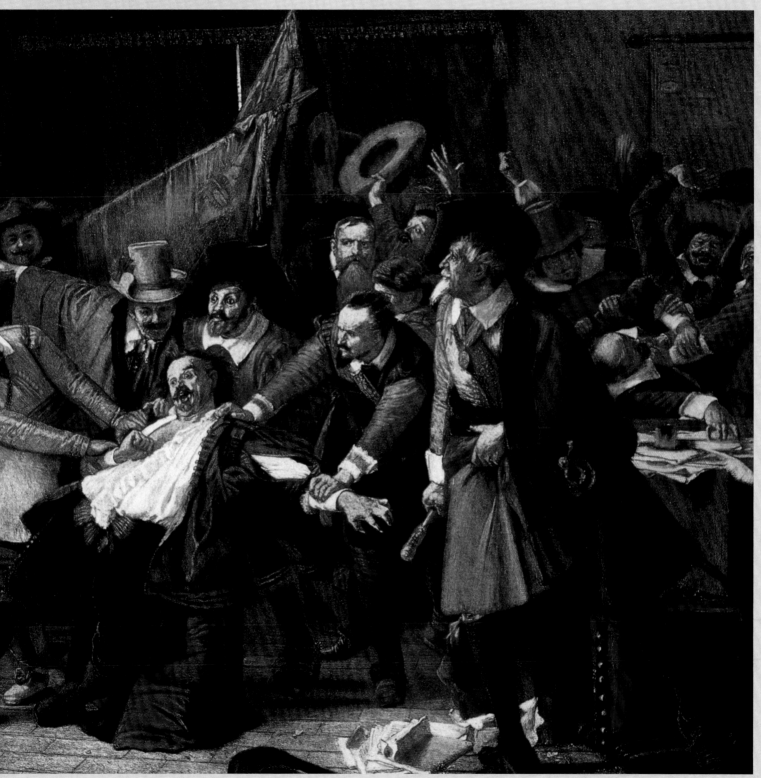

NOVÝ SVĚT, POHOŘELEC

Two areas characterize the northern and southern parts of the Hradčany District: located on its northern edges is Nový Svět, a settlement with picturesque lanes and alleyways that was not built until the 16th century and whose euphemistic name (meaning "new world") should not hide the fact that this was once a slum. On the southern periphery, the Hollow Way (Úvoz) running from east to west below the Castle, marks the boundary to the Strahov Monastery District. In its upper third the path divides, continuing southward directly to the Strahov Monastery and northward to the Pohořelec, the central square of the eponymous district, built from 1375. "Pohořelec" means "the scene of fire" – and indeed this area was burned down not just once but several times in its history, most recently in 1742, when Prague was under siege during the War of the Austrian Succession.

Here "you live only until the house is demolished or you are evicted, albeit on historical ground", said Franz Werfel. Today the Hradčany District presents itself as a charming mixture of small, simple houses, many a souvenir shop, as well as a few magnificent palaces. Although most houses were altered in the 18th and 19th centuries, time seems to have stood still here much earlier than that.

STRAHOV MONASTERY (STRAHOVSKÝ KLÁŠTER)

The name of this Premonstratensian monastery, founded in 1143, means "guardian" – and indeed, this was not only a place where god was venerated in quiet contemplation but also a fortified complex, which formed an additional defence to Prague Castle on the eastern side. During the course of its long history, the complex was devastated several times by fire during wars, but each time it was rebuilt even more magnificently than before. The monastery was not given its present appearance until the middle of the 18th century. The Monastery Church of the Virgin Mary's Ascension also underwent a make-over; originally a three-aisled Romanesque basilica church, it was refashioned in the baroque style and completed in about 1750. Proudly it is pointed out to visitors that, during the course of a visit to Prague, Wolfgang Amadeus Mozart played the church's organ here in 1787.

STRAHOV MONASTERY (STRAHOVSKÝ KLÁŠTER)

The Order of the Premonstratensians, founded in 1120 by Norbert of Xanten as a reformed church, emerged during a period when many people felt that the Church had become alienated from the spirit of the Gospel. Among the precious manuscripts kept in the monastery (left, an exterior view; below left the Theological Library Hall; right the ceiling fresco in the Summer Refectory) is the Strahov Evangeliar (9th/10th century).

AUTHOR, CIVIL RIGHTS ACTIVIST, PRESIDENT: VÁCLAV HAVEL

"Thank you, Václav", were the words on a banner when more than 10,000 people accompanied the late "poet-president's" funeral procession through the inner city of Prague in December 2011 to pay their last respects. Václav Havel, born in Prague in 1936, had made a name for himself not only as a writer but also as a civil rights activist and a critic of the communist regime. His involvement earned him several prison terms, for example in the runup to the "Prague Spring", when the attempt to establish "socialism with a human face" was nipped in the bud by Warsaw Pact troops invading the country in August 1968. Nevertheless, as the initiator of the "Charter 77" civil rights movement, Havel also helped pave the way for the "Velvet Revolution", which led to the fall of the old government in 1989. In the December of that same year, representatives of the Federal Assembly nominated the activist as a presidential candidate and in July 1990, in the first free elections to have taken place in the country for 40 years, he was confirmed in office. Havel was the president of the Czech Republic from 1993, when Slovakia split from the Czech republic to become an independent country, until 2003. His legacy (formulated in 1989 during a demonstration on Wenceslas Square) is unforgettable: "Truth and Love must prevail over Lies and Hatred."

AUTHOR, CIVIL RIGHTS ACTIVIST, PRESIDENT: VÁCLAV HAVEL

"The face of Czech freedom" ("Die Zeit" newspaper): Václav Havel was awarded the Peace Prize of the German Book Trade in 1989; in the same year, as the cofounder and speaker of a citizens' forum, he became a key figure in the "Velvet Revolution", promoting democratic change. Below Havel can be seen in his Prague office and on the Castle's balcony, left during a book signing session in New York.

LESSER TOWN (MALÁ STRANA)

As early as the eighth century, a settlement was established at the foot of the Castle Hill, and by the middle of the 13th century the village had grown so large that it was granted a town charter in 1257. Unlike the Old Town, on the opposite bank of the Vltava, this district became known as the "civitas minor pragensis", the "lesser Prague town", and it is today referred to as "Lesser Town" or sometimes "Little Quarter". A ford and later a bridge connected the Lesser Town with the Old Town. Destroyed several times by fire, the district was to become ever more attractive after each reconstruction.

View of Charles Bridge and the turrets of the
Lesser Town, "whose quiet, secretive alleyways
are full of poetic corners", as described by Jan
Neruda in his "Tales of the Lesser Town".
"Here", he wrote, "houses like people possess
something dignified, ... also something sleepy".

THE RIVER, THE KING, HIS WIFE AND HER LOVER

The Vltava River's main sources rise in the Bohemian Forest and the Bavarian Forest. After a course of just under 440 km (274 mi), in the central Bohemian town of Melnik, it flows into the Elbe River, making it Bohemia's only river to be linked with the North Sea. Inseparably linked with the Vltava and Prague is the fate of the Bohemian priest John of Nepomuk, the vicar-general at Prague Castle during the reign of Wenceslas IV. In 1393, he chose torture rather than revealing to the jealous king the name of his wife Sophie's lover, whose father confessor he was. Nepomuk did not survive the torture, and the enraged king had the corpse dismembered and thrown from a bridge into river during the gloomy night of March 20. Legend knows two versions of what happened next, but in each of these, a miracle happens: according to the first version, the corpse was allegedly recovered because the Vltava dried out all of a sudden. According to the other version, the queen had a vision in which five twinkling stars (standing for the five letters of Latin "tacui" – "I kept silent") revealed to her the place where the body parts of the drowned man could be found. In 1400, Nepomuk's remains were transferred to St Vitus Cathedral; in 1719, he was exhumed and apparently his tongue was found fully preserved; and in 1729 he was canonized by Pope Benedict XIII.

THE RIVER, THE KING, HIS WIFE AND HER LOVER

The Vltava is also known as the "Bohemian Sea". Coming from the south, it flows through Prague in a northerly direction and continues, enclosing the Old Town in a large eastbound loop. It is crossed by fifteen bridges within the city limits, and at the level of the inner city there are several islands created by sediment. In winter, many waterfowl find a refuge on these islands and on the riverbanks.

CHARLES BRIDGE (KARLŮV MOST)

CHARLES BRIDGE (KARLŮV MOST)

Between 1158 and 1172, King Vladislav II had the first stone bridge within the confines of present-day Prague built across the Vltava, replacing an older wooden bridge that had been swept away by high waters. It was named Judith Bridge after the king's second wife, Judith of Thuringia. However, this stone bridge was itself damaged so badly by high waters that Charles IV ordered the construction of yet another bridge, which was built from 1357. Modeled architecturally on a bridge in the German city of Regensburg and called simply "Stone Bridge", the new bridge measured just under 520 m (1,706 ft) in length and 10 m (33 ft) in width. In order to render it as solid as possible, it was supported by a total of 16 stone pillars. The pillars rest on enormous foundations shaped like ships' hulls, which additionally provide protection from ice floes and tree trunks floating in the river's waters.

CHARLES BRIDGE (KARLŮV MOST)

On July 9, 1357, in fact exactly at 05.31 a.m., Charles IV laid the foundation stone for the structure which was eventually to be named after him, but not until 1870. Date and time were not accidental – they had been determined as auspicious by the royal court astrologers. The magic of numbers also played a role here: the numerical sequence of 1357, 9, 7, 5, 31 formed a symmetrical, rising and falling line.

CHARLES BRIDGE (KARLŮV MOST)

With the exception of a crucifix that had been erected in the 14th century, Charles Bridge had no figurative decoration until the final third of the 17th century. It was only then that the bridge developed into a display stage for sculptures. Most of the thirty statues standing on both sides of the bridge have now been replaced by replicas; however, this does not at all affect the charm of this predominantly baroque ensemble, which also forms an interesting contrast with the gothic architecture of the bridge itself. The start was made with the figure of St John of Nepomuk, dating from 1683, whose head is crowned by five stars in allusion to the saint's legend. In 1938, St Cyrill and St Methodius were added as the final group. Most of the sculptures were erected in the 18th century, and were donated by the Church, the City of Prague and universities, all of which were competing for the honor.

Most of the originals of the statues on this "sculptural stage" (left) are today kept at the National Museum's Lapidarium and on the Vyšehrad, the city's second, southerly castle hill. The original 14th-century bronze crucifix was replaced in 1629; in 1666, two further statues were added, but these were replaced by the present statues of the Virgin Mary and John the Evangelist (below) in 1861.

CHARLES BRIDGE (KARLŮV MOST)

Both ends of the Charles Bridge are marked by bridge towers: the two Lesser Town bridge towers in the west and the Old Town bridge tower in the east. The more recent and taller bridge tower in the Lesser Town was commissioned by King George of Poděbrad in 1464, and built in the place of an earlier Romanesque structure; between 1879 and 1883 it was refashioned in the gothic style. The older and shorter tower was built in the final quarter of the 12th century, and once formed a part of the earlier Judith Bridge. It too was transformed in 1591. The crenellated gate between the two towers was probably built around the same time as the Charles Bridge. The Old Town tower on the east side dates from 1357, the work of Peter Parler. Regarded as outstanding thanks to its sculptures, it is a superb example of secular gothic art. Partly completed by Parler's successors, it is still largely intact.

The lower, older of the two Lesser Town bridge towers is also known as "Judith Tower", after Judith Bridge, a precursor to Charles Bridge. Below, the tower and dome of St Nicholas Church can be seen between the two Lesser Town towers. When comparing the two pictures, it becomes clear that the taller of the two towers had been planned as an architectural counterpoint to the Old Town bridge tower (left).

THE EMPEROR AND HIS CITY: CHARLES IV

Charles IV (1316–1378) was born into the house of Luxembourg – a German ducal dynasty, which together with the Habsburgs supplied most of the Roman German kings in the Late Middle Ages. Christened Wenceslas, he was the son of John the Blind, King of Bohemia (1311–1346), and his wife Elizabeth, a member of the Přemyslid dynasty and the second oldest daughter of King Wenceslas II. In 1346, Charles IV was nominated king of the Romans, and a year later king of Bohemia; in 1355 he became the Holy Roman Emperor. Born in Prague (where he also died), Charles IV loved "his" city, which at the time counted around 40,000 inhabitants, making it one of the largest in Europe. He promoted Prague as best he could, making it the political, cultural and economic heart of the Holy Roman Empire. Charles also persuaded the Pope to make the city an archbishops' see, and he laid the foundation stone for the building of St Vitus Cathedral on the Hradčany. A rather daring town planning project for his day was the building of the so-called New Town, from around 1348, which created homes designed for small merchants, artisans and day laborers. In the New Town's central square, today's Charles Square, the king exhibited each year for the feast of Corpus Christi the imperial crown jewels that were otherwise kept in Karlštejn Castle.

In 1356, Charles IV published the "Golden Bull" (left), which served as the basic law for the Holy Roman Empire until the year 1806. The historicizing mural (before 1841) by Johann Franz Brentano (below right), hanging in the Imperial Hall of the Römer, Frankfurt's town hall, shows Charles IV with the manuscript and the rulers' insignia – crown, scepter and sword. Large picture: a view of Charles Bridge.

FRANZ KAFKA MUSEUM

Aside from some journeys, periods spent at various sanatoria and some time in Berlin toward the end of his life, the writer Franz Kafka hardly ever left his native town, Prague. A love–hate relationship tied him to the city – he described it as a "little mother with claws". For him, it symbolized everything that kept him imprisoned and stopped him from dedicating himself exclusively to writing – just like his profession and his family. Prague was also the setting for the action of some of his most important works; in his novel, "The Trial", for example, a key chapter takes place in a cathedral that was clearly based on St Vitus Cathedral. During communism, Kafka was considered a persona non grata, because he did not write in the spirit of socialist realism. Today, his work has been rediscovered and newly appreciated, and the Franz Kafka Museum informs visitors about his life and literary work.

Housed in a former tile factory on the banks of the Vltava, the museum preserves the artist's legacy (left, a photograph of Doro Diamant, Kafka's last great love). Large picture: David Černý's sculptures, dating from 2004, standing in front of the museum entrance. The Prague sculptor has made his name with his ironic imagery: here two bronze men piss into a fountain shaped like the Czech Republic.

KAMPA ISLAND, VLTAVA

Kampa Island in the Vltava River is separated from the Lesser Town only by the narrow Devil's Brook, which thanks to its strong current was once used to drive the wheels of a mill. The Charles Bridge's pillars closest to the riverbank stand on this island. The name Kampa probably originated from the Latin word "campus" (meaning "field"), for in the early days several types of fruit and vegetables were indeed grown here for the city's population. Later, potters and rafters lived on the island, as well as the "icemen" who would cut large blocks out of the frozen water in winter and then sell them in the summer. After the devastating fires in the Lesser Town during the 16th century, people used the debris created by the fire in order to raise and shore up the land. The former Sova Mill in the south of the island, facing the Vltava, has been converted and today houses the Kampa Museum.

The Devil's Brook (Čertovka), built in the 12th century as a mill stream, separates Kampa Island from the Lesser Town. Houses were not built on the island until the 15th/16th century. Accessible from Charles Bridge via a staircase, the island was used to store goods until they could be taken across the bridge to the city's markets – once the toll fees had been paid.

KAMPA MUSEUM

This Museum of Modern Art goes back to an initiative by the Czech emigré and art patron Meda Mladkova, who donated the collection she had assembled together with her husband Jan to the City of Prague. The public was to have access to the collection in the converted Sova Mill on Kampa Island. Yet the project nearly failed in August 2002: the art exhibition, which had just been mounted there, had to be taken down again and rescued from a very destructive flood. The Kampa Museum eventually opened in September 2003, receiving a special accolade when it was chosen by Google's Art Project as one of the most important art spaces in the world. Virtual access to the museum is provided via the internet, thus including its collection in the ranks of such distinguished galleries as London's Tate Britain, the Uffici in Florence and the Museum of Modern Art in New York.

Th focus of the museum's collections (far left and below left) are the paintings and drawings of František Kupka, a precursor of Czech Abstract art, as well the sculptures of Otto Gutfreund, an important representative of Czech Cubism. In addition there are works by contemporary artists such as Magdalena Abakanowicz (below right: "Figures") and David Černý (left: "Miminka" – Babies).

MOSTECKÁ STREET

At one time, the old trading route from Regensburg, Nuremberg and Leipzig to the Vltava and beyond, to eastern Europe, was formed by this street, which is the continuation of Charles Bridge. One of the main access roads to the castle, Mostecká Street was lined with inns, shops and workshops on both sides and has always been a hive of activity. Of special interest to art historians is Kaunitz Palace (Kaunický palác, at No. 15), which was built by Anton Karl Schmidt between 1730 and 1775 in the style of the Rococo-Neoclassicism. It was the home of the Yugoslav Embassy and now houses the Embassy of Serbia. Also worth seeing is Saxon House (at No. 3), a stately building gifted to the Saxon Duke Rudolf by Charles IV in 1348, after which it became the Prague residence of the Saxon dukes until 1408. On the south side of the bridge approach is the former Lesser Town bridge toll office (at No. 1).

Today, the trappings of global tourism – souvenir shops and fast-food restaurants – dominate the appearance of Mostecká Street (left). Yet some well-preserved structures testify to the former glory of the street, such as the remains of a gothic episcopal palace in the courtyard of the house at No. 16. At the end of the street rise the Lesser Town bridge towers (below left; below right, the arch linking the two towers).

LESSER TOWN SQUARE (MALOSTRANSKÉ NÁMĚSTÍ)

Lesser Town Square is spread out between Mostecká Street and Neruda Street, along the old coronation route of the Bohemian kings leading up to Prague Castle. Since the 10th century, this has been the heart of the Lesser Town. At that time, a regular market was already held here, and a Romanesque church dedicated to St Wenceslas as well as several other buildings stood in the square. Since 1238, it has been divided into an upper and a lower section by a gothic parish church, dedicated to St Nicholas. Liechtenstein Palace (Lichtenštejnský palác) stands opposite, on its west side; it was created by combining five splendid manor houses into a single one. In the 1620s, the palace served as a residence for Karl von Liechtenstein, the chief chamberlain of the Catholic emperor Rudolf II who ruled from Vienna and entered the annals of Prague's history as a particularly fanatical scourge of the Protestants.

LESSER TOWN SQUARE (MALOSTRANSKÉ NÁMĚSTÍ)

On the Royal Route from the Hradčany Hill to the New Town, a tram crosses Lesser Town Square. Almost all the surrounding buildings conceal behind their Renaissance, baroque or Empire façades a medieval core. Some of the typical passageways and halfway houses have been preserved especially on the south side of the elongated square. Today they house a great variety of different shops.

ST NICHOLAS CHURCH, LESSER TOWN (CHRÁM SVATÉHO MIKULÁŠE)

The vast size of the Church of St Nicholas, Prague's largest baroque church built in the place of an earlier gothic structure of the same name, is explained by the fact that it was erected in the 17th and 18th centuries, at the time of the Counter-Reformation and the restoration of the Catholic Church in the Bohemian lands. The power and the glory of its architecture, created under the direction of three generations of the best master-builders in Prague, were at the same time meant to mirror the triumph of orthodox Catholicism over the deviationist doctrines of the Protestants. During the communist era, the church was put to service for a political ideology. The palaces located at the foot of the Hradčany, where many western countries, including the United States, had their embassies, were being observed from the roughly 80-m-tall (262-ft) bell tower – an open secret in Prague.

ST NICHOLAS CHURCH, LESSER TOWN (CHRÁM SVATÉHO MIKULÁŠE)

Soon after the victory of the Catholics in the Battle of White Mountain (1625), Ferdinand II of Habsburg passed the parish Church of St Nicholas, dating from 1238, to the Lesser Town Jesuits. In 1673, the foundation stone was laid for a new church in the presence of Emperor Leopold I. It was built by the father and son duo Christoph and Kilian Ignaz Dientzenhofer. Anselmo Lurago completed the belltower in 1756.

ST THOMAS (KOSTEL SVATÉHO TOMÁŠE), ST JOSEPH (SVATÝ JOSEFH)

The Church of St Thomas, situated to the north-east of Lesser Town Square, is a three-aisled Romanesque basilica. Construction was begun as early as 1285 by the Augustinian hermits, an order founded by King Wenceslas II; the church was not completed, however, until 1379. Later generations converted it again and again – after a fire and while reconstructing it during the time of the Hussite wars, for example, as well as during its transformation into the palace church ordered by Emperor Rudolf II in the 16th century. Its present appearance dates back to the baroque makeover by Kilian Ignaz Dientzenhofer between 1725 and 1731. Nearby, the baroque Church of St Joseph was also originally attached to a Carmelite convent. It was founded much later, however, in 1656. Its main altar is adorned with a depiction of the Holy Family by Peter Johannes Brandl.

ST THOMAS (KOSTEL SVATÉHO TOMÁŠE), ST JOSEPH (SVATÝ JOSEFH)

Scenes from the lives of the father of the order, St Augustine, as well as of St Thomas, are depicted in the ceiling frescoes in the nave of St Thomas (below center; below left and right the choir), the work of the Prague painter Václav Vavřinec Reiner in 1728. The Church of St Joseph (left) was built in the Flemish baroque style in 1687 to 1692 (left), featuring a two-level façade.

NERUDOVA STREET

Nerudova Street, forming the final section of the former Royal Route of the Bohemian kings, has been lined by a multitude of splendid buildings since the days of the Baroque. Starting on Lesser Town Square and leading rather steeply up Castle Hill, it was known as "Spur Street" until it was renamed in honor of the writer Jan Neruda (1834–1891). Neruda lived here from 1845 to 1857, in the "House of the Two Suns" – his name, incidentally, was apparently adopted as a pseudonym by the Chilean Nobel Prize of Literature winner, Pablo Neruda (real name: Neftalí Ricardo Reyes Basoalto). Nerudova Street is a lively lane with many shops and cafés. Two of its most attractive secular buildings were built by the Italian architect Giovanni Blasius Santini-Aichel: the Morzin Palace (c. 1713, today the Romanian Embassy) and the Thun-Hohenstein Palace (1726, today the Italian Embassy).

The writer Jan Neruda, who lived in Nerudova Street for twelve years, dedicated his "Lesser Town Tales" to the district and its inhabitants. In these stories you can read all about "Doctor Spoiler" ("whose true name was Heribert"), for example, or about, "how it came to be that Austria was not destroyed on August 20, 1849, at 12.30 lunchtime".

SYMBOLS AND MIRACLES

"The Lesser Town is the quietest district of Prague", said the German lyric poet Detlev von Liliencron (an "emissary of great German poetry", who, according to Max Brod, significantly influenced the so-called Prague School), adding: "There are still places here where the grass grows between the cobble stones, and in the evening especially, some streets create the impression as if they belonged to a peaceful landscape of a very venerable age." The latter – the bit about the venerable age – is also true about the symbolic imagery that was once used to provide an orientation aid for the medieval pedestrian in this otherwise disorientating city, and which today you can still hardly miss on your stroll through the streets of Prague. Numerous façades are adorned with house symbols – cast in bronze, painted onto the plaster or engraved in stone – , which allowed everyone to guess at the profession, faith, name or origins of each house's occupants. It was not until 1770, during the reign of Empress Maria Theresa (and following the French model, introduced to facilitate the work of the recruiting officers in the army) that the house were first given numbers. Two types of numbers at that: orientation numbers (the equivalent of today's house numbers) and conscription numbers (referring to the districts, such as Old Town, Hradčany or Lesser Town).

Unfortunately, over time, the meaning of many of the house symbols in Prague, which today have been lovingly restored, has been forgotten. It is known, however, that the famous "Three Little Fiddles" (bottom right) at No. 12 Neruda Street indicate that the Edlingers, a family of violin makers, lived here from 1667 to 1748. At No. 49 Neruda Street you can find the house of the "White Swan" (below left).

NEW CASTLE STAIRS (NOVÉ ZÁMECKÉ SCHODY)

The shortest and most attractive route from the Lesser Town to the Castle is via the New Castle Stairs. Initially, the stairs run parallel to Neruda Street, thus giving the stroller an opportunity also to admire the back of the hillside row of houses. This parallel route is also accessible by taking the small built-over passageway below the Italian Embassy in the Thun-Hohenstein Palace (at No. 20 Nerudova Street). The central section of the New Castle Stairs is marked by the Slavata Palace, built in the 16th century and whose southern wing originally was the Thun-Hohenstein Palace. Not set in stone, but unforgotten in literary terms is the "smell of Pilsener beer ... and sausages with horseradish", as described by the essayist Alfred Kerr, that once wafted to your nose "at the foot of the Castle district, where the path climbs up to the Bohemian Acropolis".

This access route from the Lesser Town to the Castle was made up of stairs already in the 15th century. During the ascent, the displays of artisans and craftspeople who had their shops here could be admired. They presented their wares on the mighty sills of windows set far back in the walls. To experience the New Castle Stairs at their most idyllic, as below, time your visit for early morning or late night.

WALLENSTEIN PALACE (VALDŠTEJNSKÝ PALÁC)

It is debatable whether this palace is one of the most magnificent baroque aristocratic residences in the world or rather a monument in stone to the self-importance of its architect. For in 1623, the famous (and infamous) imperial generalissimo Prince Albrecht of Valdštejn (1583–1634, known as Wallenstein or Waldstein, and whose rise and fall was told in Schiller's Wallenstein trilogy) had more than 20 houses and an entire brick factory demol-ished and several gardens flattened, just to create space for his new "home, sweet home". No wonder then, that the general, who by his marriages had accumulated incredible wealth, was hated by the general public and also incurred the displeasure of the ruling monarch. His giant edifice could not be missed when looking down from the Castle, a fact that could only be interpreted as an architectural declaration of war against the monarch.

WALLENSTEIN PALACE (VALDŠTEJNSKÝ PALÁC)

"Do not take half measures", must have been the motto when this monumental palace was built, the first in the Prague baroque style, to the designs of Andrea Spezza and Giovanni Pieroni. The general was murdered on the orders of Emperor Ferdinand II because of his unauthorized actions during a banquet in 1634. Golo Mann wrote that, in the middle of the big city, Wallenstein had tried to create "a miniature empire".

A VISION OF PRAGUE: PALACE GARDEN (PALÁCOVÉ ZAHRADY)

"I had a vision", said the American writer Julien Green, "and it was Prague. I departed from one period of time in order to enter the past." Walking along Valdštejnská Street in a northerly direction from the Wallenstein Palace, it is still like that today: "One ambles – although this may be thought hardly possible – through another epoch, for this city is so otherworldly that it seems unreal." Here it is baroque Prague that is still highly present even today – at No. 14, for example, stands the Pálffy Palace, which now serves as an academy of music; at No. 10, the Kolowrat Palace, which houses an outpost of the Ministery of Culture; at No. 8, the Fürstenberg Palace, where the Polish Embassy is based; and at No. 3, you will have reached the Ledebour Palace located on Wallenstein Square (Valdštejnská náměstí). All these palaces, most of which were built in the 18th century, still boast magnificent gardens behind their baroque façades, climbing up the southern slopes to Prague Castle in terraces. Boasting a large number of arches and balustrades, galleries and statues, fountains, pavilions and temples, the gardens are often more interesting than the palaces themselves. A good place then, to recall Julien Green again, who at the end of his time travels said that now he had arrived "in Prague time, beyond our hourly zones".

A VISION OF PRAGUE: PALACE GARDEN (PALÁCOVÉ ZAHRADY)

At first, for strategic reasons, Prague's Castle Hill was left bare. It was not until the reign of Charles IV that vineyards were established there, and in the 18th century these were transformed into baroque works of horticultural art. Today, the Fürstenberg Garden (far left) and the Great Pálffy Garden (left) are a feast to behold, and the Ledebour Palace (large picture) boasts a splendid Sala Terrena (level garden room).

LOBKOWICZ PALACE (LOBKOVICKÝ PALÁC)

On December 11, 1973, "the Treaty on mutual relations between the Federal Republic of Germany and the Czechoslovak Socialist Republic" was signed, "in the historic awareness that the harmonious coexistence of the nations in Europe is a necessity for peace ..." (thus the first words of said treaty). The treaty was the basis for the resumption of diplomatic relations between the two states, which happened on that same day. As the seat for the German Embassy in Prague, the Lobkowicz Palace was chosen – not a bad choice, for this was one of the most beautiful baroque palaces in the city. Constructed in the years 1703 to 1713 and to the designs of the Italian architect Giovanni Battista Alliprandi, its present appearance dates back to an alteration in the year 1769, following the plans of Ignaz Palliardi, during which the two side tracts were also raised in height.

LOBKOWICZ PALACE (LOBKOVICKÝ PALÁC)

History in the making: "We have come to you to tell you that today, your departure is now possible." With these words – the last ones drowned out by tumultuous cheers – with which the German Foreign Minister at the time, Hans-Dietrich Genscher, announced on September 30, 1989, on the garden balcony of Lobkowicz Palace, that nearly 4,000 refugees from the GDR would be allowed to leave the country.

VRTBA PALACE (VRTBOVSKÝ PALÁC), VRTBA GARDEN (VRTBOVSKÁ ZAHRADA)

Walking from Lobkowicz Palace in an easterly direction toward Karmelitská Street – today the main traffic artery in the Lesser Town –, you will get to the Vrtba Palace (Vrtbovský palác) at No. 25, on the corner of Tržiště. It was created in the years 1627 to 1631 by combining two town houses. The northern house previously belonged to Christoph Harant von Polschitz und Weseritz, one of the most important Bohemian composers, who was beheaded as one of the Protestant rebels during the "Day of Blood" (June 21, 1621). The new owner of the manor house, Sezima of Vrtba, had the narrow passageway between the amalgamated houses faced by a portal; the alleyway itself, however, remained intact. Through the passage, visitors gain access to the Vrtba Garden, one of the most beautiful baroque gardens in central Europe, laid out to the plans of František Maximilián Kaňka.

VRTBA PALACE (VRTBOVSKÝ PALÁC), VRTBA GARDEN (VRTBOVSKÁ ZAHRADA)

Prague's enthusiasm for all things baroque also manifested itself in horticultural designs. When in 1541 a fire devastated large areas of the Lesser Town, the aristocrats commissioned "magical gardens" for themselves on the slopes close to the Castle and on Petřin Hill: "... a sort of open-air theater, dug into the side of the hill, divided into round terraces and adorned by statues of great beauty" (D. Fernandez).

CHURCH OF OUR LADY VICTORIOUS (KOSTEL PANNY MARIE VÍTĚZNÉ)

It is less than five minutes on foot walking southward from the Vrtba Palace down Karmelitská Street to the city's oldest preserved baroque church. Built by Giovanni M. Filippi between 1611 and 1613 on the orders of the German Lutherans, its plan was based on the Jesuit church "Il Gesù" in Rome. After the Battle of White Mountain in 1620, the church was transferred to the Order of the Discalced (or Barefoot) Carmelites, who dedicated it to Our Lady of Victory on January 8, 1624 ("Maria de Victoria"). There was a reason for this, of course, for choosing this name: legend has it that one of the monks of the order, after whom the Karmelitská Street is also named, preceded the Catholic troops during the Battle of White Mountain, carrying a devotional image and thus proving for all time that (blind) faith is not only able to move mountains but also to win battles.

CHURCH OF OUR LADY VICTORIOUS (KOSTEL PANNY MARIE VÍTĚZNÉ)

In 1628, the Carmelites were gifted a 47-cm-tall (19-inch) wax statuette by the Countess Polyxena Lobkowicz, who herself had received the statue from her mother, the Spanish Duchess Maria Maxmiliana (Marie) Manrique de Lara. The "Prague Infant Jesus" is credited with a number of miracles – such as the expulsion of the Swedes who had abandoned their "righteous faith" from the town on the Vltava in 1648.

PETŘIN HILL

A small passageway behind the gardens of the Lobkowicz Palace leads to the Petřin, an eastern foothill of the White Mountain that was originally densely wooded. Vines were cultivated on its slopes from the 12th to the 19th centuries, and thereafter it became one of the most attractive recreation areas close to the city center – Kafka already sat "on the backrest of the Petřin Hill, ... examining the wishes [he] had for life". The Czech name is said by Bohemia's first chronicler, Cosmas of Prague (c. 1045–1125) to have been derived from the Latin word for rock ("petra"). Its German name, Laurenziberg, refers to the Roman martyr Laurentius, the patron saint of the church on the summit. Remains of the "hunger wall" recall the old city fortifications, allegedly built on the orders of Charles IV during the famine of about 1360, in order to give the city's poor a wage and thus something to eat.

From Petřin Hill, just under 320 m (1,050 ft) high, the views extend far across the city and beyond (below). Visitors finding the ascent too arduous can take the funicular railway instead (left). Anyone regarding the hill as not high enough, can climb the 60-m-tall (197-ft) viewing tower. Built in 1891 as a miniature version of the Eiffel Tower and moved here in 1930, it affords views as far as the country's borders in fine weather.

OLD TOWN (STARÉ MĚSTO) AND JEWISH QUARTER (JOSEFOV)

Merchants and artisans settled on the right bank of the Vltava early on, as it was protected by fortresses in the north-west (Hradčany) and in the south-east (Vyšehrad). In 1235, King Wenceslas I granted the town charter to this always prosperous market town, and in the 14th century, during Charles IV's reign, the "Old Town of Prague" developed into one of the most important towns of the Middle Ages. The Jewish population lived in their own district, also known as the "fifth quarter" and renamed Josefov (Joseph's Town) in the 18th century, after Emperor Joseph II, who had granted them certain freedoms.

Around Old Town Square, the medieval structure of Prague has been largely preserved to the present day. This settlement was an important center for trade as early as about 965, as is documented in a report by the emissary of the Caliph of Córdoba in southern Spain.

KNIGHTS OF THE CROSS SQUARE (KŘIŽOVNICKÉ NÁMĚSTÍ)

Relatively small, but thanks to its harmonious architecture very impressive, this square featuring a statue of Charles IV was named after the order of the "Knights of the Cross with the Red Star". The order originated in the 13th century from a charitable fraternity of laymen; it is the only spiritual knight order founded in Bohemia, and it is also the only monastic order ever to have been founded by a woman. The woman in question was Agnes of Bohemia (1211–1282), proclaimed a saint in 1989 and the youngest daughter of Přemysl Ottokar I and Constance of Hungary – which certainly contributed to the fact that the order enjoyed protection from high up. In 1253, the Knights of the Cross settled on the banks of the Vltava where the Judith Bridge still stood at that time, the stone precursor of the present Charles Bridge. Here they soon established a church and a hospital.

From 1561 to 1694, the archbishops of Prague all came from the order of the Knights of the Cross. Their might led to a dispute with the influential Jesuits. One visible sign of this power struggle is the enormous dome of the Knights of the Cross Church, built from 1679 to 1689 (left, view from Charles Bridge and internal view), which "triumphed" over the Jesuit St Salvator Church (below right in the picture).

CLEMENTINUM (KLEMENTINUM)

Ferdinand I invited the Jesuits to Prague in 1556 in order to create a focus for the Counter-Reformation, with their assistance – and also a bulwark against the university which promoted the humanities as well as the sciences. To this end, an abandoned Dominican monastery that had been devastated during the Hussite wars, was given to the Jesuits. Located between Knights of the Cross Square and St Mary's Square, the knights built a Catholic college in its place. The king himself sent his noble sons there, and the fathers were soon granted the right to award doctorates (which placed them in direct competition with Prague University). With the support of other pro-Catholic patrons, the Clementinum was expanded, and by 1726 it had become Prague's second-largest structure (after the Castle) – an entire city district had to be demolished to make room for it.

CLEMENTINUM (KLEMENTINUM)

In addition to residential halls for teachers and students, and seminar and lecture halls, the Clementinum, located close to the banks of the Vlatava, also housed a theater and print works, an observatory and, last but not least, several churches, as well as the Mirror Chapel (below right). Today it is the home of the Czech National Library (left; below left, the baroque library hall, which boasts a number of valuable globes).

MY QUAY, MY MUSIC, MY FATHERLAND: SMETANA

After the foundation of the first Czech Republic (on October 28, 1918), the "Franz Quay", running alongside the Vltava and whose name now carried unwanted associations with the Austrian rulers, was renamed after the composer Bedřich Smetana (1824–1884). It was an obvious choice: Smetana's best-known work, the second part of his set of six symphonic poems, "My Fatherland" (Má Vlast, 1882), which premiered in Prague on November 5, 1882, is entitled "The Vltava". With it, Smetana had created a musical monument for the "Czech national river". The composer was a proud patriot who had joined the national movement to fight against domination by the centralized power in Vienna and who for his work often drew on themes from Bohemian history and mythology. In his opera "Dalibor" (1868), for example, Smetana made his story around the fate of a nobleman who is said to have languished in a tower named after him, the Daliborka Tower, in Golden Lane. Another one of Smetana's operas, "Libuše" (1881), has as its subject the legendary founder mother of the Přemyslid ruling dynasty. A museum dedicated to the composer's life and work is housed in a former waterworks, at the northern end of Smetana Quay; a statue of the great man stands in front of the museum – appropriately with his gaze directed toward the Vltava.

MY QUAY, MY MUSIC, MY FATHERLAND: SMETANA

Smetana (below left, painted portrait) was originally christened Friedrich. It was only when he had become an adult that he decided to use the Czech equivalent of his first name, Bedřich, and then began to learn and use the Czech language. Large picture below right: the Smetana statue in front of the museum dedicated to the composer, on Smetana Quay. Left: a particularly atmospheric view of "his" quay.

CHARLES STREET (KARLOVA)

If the old maxim still holds true, that the customer is king, then not a lot has changed in Charles Street for the last few hundreds of years. Today it is still "kings" who stroll along the cobbled street, a section of the former Royal Route of the Bohemian kings – however, there are very many more such strollers than in earlier days, and they now have to first step into one of the many shops lining both sides of the route in order to – hopefully – be treated like a crowned head of state. Back on the cobbles of Charles Street, visitors should take the time to have a look at the beautiful details on the house fronts – to admire the Colloredo Mansfeld Palace (No. 2 Karlova), for example, on the corner of Smetana Quay, where they should also take in the Neptune fountain in the courtyard, or the house "To the Golden Fountain" (at No. 3 Charles Street) with its superb baroque stucco relief.

The Royal Road of the Bohemian kings ran from the Powder Tower through Celetná Lane, Old Town Square, Charles Street and across the Charles Bridge to Bridge Lane, then on to Lesser Town Square and into Neruda Street in front of the Castle, with the St Vitus Cathedral as the final destination. In Charles Street, many gothic houses – later adorned with baroque decorations – are preserved, on Romanesque foundations.

CLAM-GALLAS PALACE (CLAM-GALLASŮV PALÁC)

At the corner of Hus Lane (No. 20), Mariánské Square and Charles Street stands the Clam-Gallas Palace, one of the most attractive secular buildings in the city. It was named after Jan Václav Count Gallas (1669–1719), the imperial governor-general of Prague, who in 1707 commissioned no lesser person than the famous imperial court architect, Johann Bernhard Fischer von Erlach, with the design of his city residence. Construction management for the four-winged, two-storey baroque prestige building, built on an irregular plan and boasting two inner courtyards, was entrusted to Domenico Canevale and Thomas Haffenecker. The count himself, however, is unlikely to have spent much time at his palace – in 1714 he became the vice-king of Naples and he held this office until his death. Since 1945, the palace has been the home of Prague's municipal archives.

The excellent pair of giants on the portals were created in the workshop of Matthias Bernhard Braun, and Carlo Carlone painted the frescoes on the stairs (below). Fancy-dress events (left) recall the time when glittering balls were still held at the palace, events that Mozart and his wife Constanze are also said to have enjoyed. The palace was also a venue for concerts held by renowned musicians, such as Beethoven.

PRAGUE PUPPETRY: ARTISTS ON A STRING

Puppet theaters look back on a long tradition in the city on the Vltava. Plays performed with puppets were popularized by itinerant German, English, Dutch and Italian players, who visited Bohemia as early as the 18th century, entertaining their audiences with handmade puppets and imaginatively told stories. As a rule they had a set of 12 puppets on a string – six male and three female characters, Kaspárek (a clown), Death and the Devil –, into whom they breathed life with their skilled hands. During the 19th century, Prague developed into one of the most important centers of puppetry, and this tradition, passed on from one generation to the next, is still unbroken today. In 1922, the Union Internationale de la Marionette (UNIMA) was founded in the city, the worldwide association of puppeteers. Since 1945, Prague has been the home of the Spejbl & Hurvínek puppet theater, founded as early as 1930 by Josef Skupa in Pilsen and named after its most famous protagonists. This theater has presented its artistic puppet plays in more than 250 premieres, and international guest performances have taken the great puppeteers into 31 countries so far. In 1991, the National Marionette Theater was also founded in Prague. It has become famous for its more than 4,500 performances of the Mozart opera "Don Giovanni" with (life-sized) puppets.

PRAGUE PUPPETRY: ARTISTS ON A STRING

"You have to feel the puppets", said Pavel Truhlar, "and then they will speak to you." At first, he sold his hand-carved marionettes (below left and right; center, the shop of Obchod Pod Lampou) on Charles Bridge. In 1992, Truhlar opened his first shop and today he employs some 40 puppet makers. Left: the National Marionette Theater also houses a small museum.

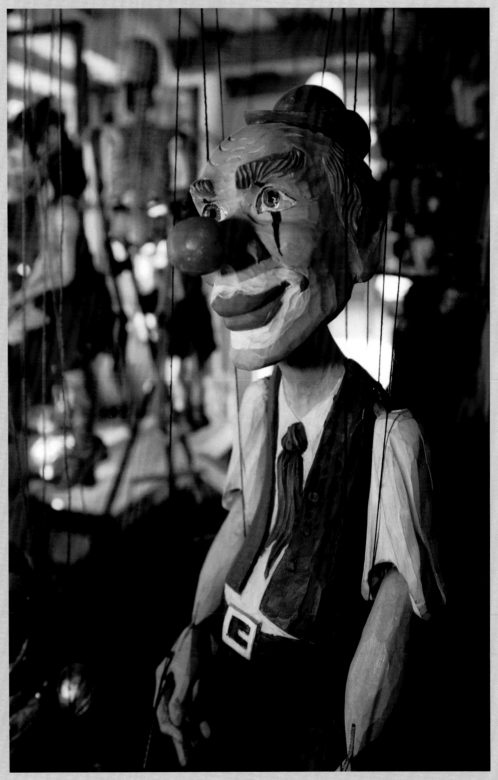

CHURCH OF ST GILES (KOSTEL SVATÉHO JILJÍ)

The three-aisled church, built on the site of an earlier structure, is noticeable from afar thanks to its twin-towered western façade, which features twin towers of different heights. Inside the church, which has its entrance on Hus Lane, there is a further peculiarity: a flat-roofed eastern end without choir, reminiscent of early Christian churches. St Giles was built in 1310 to 1371, on the orders of the Bishop of Prague, Jan IV of Dražice. During his stay at the Papal court of Avignon, Jan experienced the French gothic style and learned to love it. From 1365, Jan Milič of Kroměřiž preached at the church, a precursor to Jan Hus who himself stood in the pulpit between 1402 and 1413. In 1626, the Dominicans moved in. As part of their alterations and renovations, they had the central nave painted with a representation of their order's triumph over the "heretics" – that is to say, the Hussites.

CHURCH OF ST GILES (KOSTEL SVATÉHO JILJÍ)

In its external appearance, the church looks rather severe, in accordance with the ideals of the Bohemian Gothic. The late-baroque transformation of the interior could be regarded as a deliberate contrast, this one wholly within the spirit of the Dominicans, who moved in after the Hussites. Their plans were probably drawn up by Kilian Ignaz Dientzenhofer, and executed during the 1730s by František Špaček.

GALL TOWN (HAVELSKÉ MĚSTO)

Today's Rytířská, Havelská, Ovocný trh (fruit market) and Uhelný trh (cabbage market) streets and squares once formed an Old Town district of their own, the Gallus or Gall Town. The district is documented as early as 1235 – when Eberhard, King Vaclav I Přemysl's Master of the Mint, established the "nova civitas circa S Gallum", the new town around the Church of St Gall. At the back, building work extended to the city walls and the moat; a bridge was built to span the latter during the founding of the new town, a fact still commemorated in the street name, Na můsku (On the Little Bridge). The district, settled predominantly by colonists from southern Germany, is likely to have differed noticeably from the other quarters. It even had its own legal system until the end of the 13th century. The Church of St Gall was built at about the same time as the district, and completed in 1263.

Refashioned in the baroque style at the end of the 17th century, the Church of St Gall (left) was dedicated to St Havel, after whom the street in which it stands is also named (Havelská). Since the Middle Ages, a market (below) has been held here. At that time, a relic of the skull of St Gall was kept in the church, which had been acquired from the Swiss Monastery of St Gall. It attracted large crowds of pilgrims.

ESTATES THEATER (STAVOVSKÉ DIVADLO)

This first fixed theater building in Prague was built in the years 1781 to 1783 according to plans by the theater theoretician Count Künigl, and under the supervision of architect Anton Haffenecker. Built in the Neoclassical style, the theater was financed by Franz Anton Count Nostitz-Rieneck, the highest burgrave and deputy of the king, who had envisaged a "national spectacle in our mother tongue" (that is, in German). The playhouse opened in 1783, with a performance of Lessing's "Emilia Galotti". Toward the end of the 18th century, the Bohemian nobility purchased the building for 60,000 guilders, running it as the "Estates Theater". Architecturally modified several times by architect Achill Wolf between 1859 and 1890, it was known as Tyl Theater after 1945, named after the Czech playwright Josef Kajetán Tyl. Today it has again taken its old name and forms a part of the Czech National Theater.

"Rest I've none by night or day, / Scanty fare and doubtful pay, / Ev'ry whim I must fulfil; / Take my place whoever will!" These word by Leporello come at the beginning of Mozart's opera "Don Giovanni" which, in the words of the composer, received the "loudest applause" when it was premiered here on October 29, 1787. Two years later, another Mozart opera was first performed in this theater: "La Clemenza di Tito".

CAROLINUM (KAROLINUM)

It is said that the venerable professors of Prague University were none too pleased when the Estates Theater opened its doors right next to their noble institution. However, it is open to speculation in how far the moral ideas of the players and actors, who had moved into such close and threatening proximity and which were considered to be dubious by the professors, would indeed be able to shake the moral certitude of their students, and it is no longer possible to prove or disprove this. The facts, meanwhile, are as follows: founded on April 7, 1348, by Emperor Charles IV according to the models of Paris and Bologna, this was the first "German" university (meaning that it was attended predominantly by German students) in central Europe. The subjects of instruction at the "Collegium Carolinum" (so named after its founder) were Law, Medicine, Theology and – well, yes – the Arts.

Housed initially within several monastery buildings, the university was able to move to its own quarters in 1383. These had been put at its disposal by Wenceslas IV, the son and successor of Charles IV. At first, the medium of instruction was Latin; from the middle of the 18th century, some lectures were given in German. Jan Hus once taught Theology here. Today, more than 40,000 students are registered.

OLD TOWN HALL (STAROMĚSTSKÁ RADNICE)

Thanks to a privilege granted by King Jan of Luxembourg, who ruled in Bohemia from 1310 to 1346 and was the father of Charles IV, the citizens of the "Old Town of Prague" were permitted to set up a town hall as their own administrative center in an early-gothic building in 1338. Alterations and enlargement were financed out of the wine tax – for which the king had also granted his approval. The nesting structure of the various parts of the building clearly demonstrate how the town hall complex was continually enlarged between the 14th and 19th centuries. Today, it encompasses all the buildings between the clock tower and the "House at the Minute" adjoining in the south-west. When, in 1784, Joseph II combined all of Prague into one administrative unit, this complex of buildings in Old Town Square automatically became the seat of the new autonomous government.

OLD TOWN HALL (STAROMĚSTSKÁ RADNICE)

As a historic monument, the Old Town Hall has kept its name until today, even though only cultural and social events take place there now. In its appearance, it resembles "an archictectural historical field test with parts and elements from the most diverse periods" (Isabella Woldt). From the top of the tower, superb views of Old Town Square can be enjoyed.

FOR WHOM THE BELL TOLLS: THE MASTER, THE CLOCK AND DEATH

The Astronomical Clock (Orloj), fixed onto the south side of the nearly 70-m-tall (230-ft) tower of the Old Town Hall, was installed in about 1410 by Mikuláš z Kadaně and was completed around 1490 by Master Hanuš Růže, astronomer at Prague University. Legend tells that the councillors had Master Hanuš blinded once he had achieved his task in order to prevent him from creating a similar work of art for any other city. Shortly before his death, the cruelly blinded man is said to have climbed the tower once more to stop the clock movement. Allegedly, Jan Táborský was the only one who was able to restore the mechanism, many decades later.

The Astronomical Clock consists of three parts: at the top, the Walk of the Apostles with Christ and his Disciples, followed by the Grim Reaper who tips an hour glass at the full hour, every hour between 9 a.m. and 9 p.m.; in the middle is the clock dial (below) and at the bottom the calendar dial (right). The latter is divided into 365 day fields and advances daily by one field until it has returned back to the starting position at the end of the year. Old Czech time can be read from the clock disc in Arabic numerals (calculated from sunrise to sunset). Time as we know it, in twelve-hour cycles, can be read in Roman numerals, and the month as well as the position of the sun and moon are also displayed.

FOR WHOM THE BELL TOLLS: THE MASTER, THE CLOCK AND DEATH

The clock dial of the Astronomical Clock shows the revolutions of sun andmoon as well as time; the dial below is a calendar. Just before the full hour every hour, the famous Apostles' Walk can be seen: "Death chimes by shaking his head as he pulls the cord. Other figures move, the cock flutters and the Twelve Apostles glide past in front of the open window..." (Guillaume Apollinaire).

OLD TOWN SQUARE

The Old Town Square, covering around 9,000 sq m (96,840 sq ft) after an extension toward the Vltava in the year 1900, was laid out as early as the 11th/12th centuries as a central market square for traders. The stocks and the blood court were also here, however, and over time the square became the setting for major and often bloody events on many occasions. Thus, 27 crosses in the pavement in front of the Old Town Hall commemorate the leaders of the rebellion against the Habsburgs, who were executed here on June 21, 1621. In May 1945, the fiercest battles during the Prague Uprising for the liberation of the city raged on the square, and three years later the victory of Stalinist communism was proclaimed here. Jokingly renamed "Hyde Park" as the meeting point for the 1968 student movement, the square also played an important role during the "Velvet Revolution" of 1989.

The landmark of Prague's Old Town is the Tyn Church, whose twin towers rise above the Old Town Square, clearly visible from all sides. A church is said to have stood in the "Tyn", the district of foreign merchants, as early as the 10th century. The magnificent town houses and palaces surrounding the square attest to the prosperity of the Old Town – a wealth not restricted only to its architecture.

JAN HUS: "PRADA ZVÍTESÍ" – TRUTH PREVAILS

JAN HUS: "PRADA ZVÍTESÍ" – TRUTH PREVAILS

On his visit to Prague in 1990, the former Pope John Paul II said "I feel the need to express deep regret for the cruel death inflicted on Jan Hus and for the consequent wound of conflict and division which was thus imposed on the minds and hearts of the Bohemian people." However, the Roman Catholic Church has still not officially rehabilitated the reforming theologian, who was burned as a heretic on July 6, 1415. Born in around 1370 in the southern Bohemian town of Husinec, Hus studied at the University of Prague and became its director in 1409. As a priest, he stood behind the pulpit of the Bethlehem Chapel in Prague's Old Town until 1413. From there he spread his doctrine in front of an audience of up to 3,000 people. According to Hus, the Bible should be considered the highest religious and judicial authority, above human laws. Initially, Hus found a supporter in Václav IV, for whom the growing power of the Catholic Church was a thorn in his side, albeit for different reasons. Yet, fear of a rebellion made the king change his mind and withdraw his support for the reformer in 1412. Charged with heresy by the Council of Constance (1414–1418), Jan Hus was burned at the stake. His final words, it is said, were "Prada Zvítěsí" – Truth Prevails.

JAN HUS: "PRADA ZVÍTESÍ" – TRUTH PREVAILS

The two illustrations on the left recall the events at and after the Council of Constance. Below right: an engraving of Jan Hus by Hans Holbein the Elder, created in 1754 after a painting. Below left: Ladislav Šaloun, one of the main representatives of Czech Impressionism, was greatly influenced by the work of the French sculptor Auguste Rodin when creating his monument, erected on Old Town Square in 1915.

GOLTZ-KINSKY PALACE (PALÁC GOLTZ-KINSKÝCH)

On the eastern side of the Old Town Square stands the Goltz-Kinský Palace, completed in 1765. Its late-baroque splendor is based on the plans of Kilian Ignaz Dientzenhofer; however, the architect died in 1751, four years before construction began. The palace was commissioned by Jan Arnošt Count of Goltz and built by Anselmo Lurago (with sculptural decoration from the workshop of Ignaz Franz Platzer), on the foundations of a Romanesque and early-gothic house. Three years after completion, ownership was transferred to Count Rudolf Kinský. Just under 80 years later, the writer Bertha von Suttner was born here, a Countess of Kinský by birth, the first woman to receive the Nobel Peace Prize in 1905, for her two-volume work, "Die Waffen nieder" (1889, "Lay Down Your Arms!"). Since 2011, the palace has housed the National Gallery's Collection of Ancient and Oriental Art.

GOLTZ-KINSKY PALACE (PALÁC GOLTZ-KINSKÝCH)

From 1903, Kafka's father had a shop on the ground floor of the palace, selling ladies' wares. Two years earlier, his son had graduated from grammar school located one floor above.

In 1948, President Klement Gottwald announced the coming into force of a new, communist constitution from the palace's balcony, and in 1990, Vacláv Havel announced the end of the communist regime from the same spot.

TÝN CHURCH (KOSTEL PANNY MARIE PŘED TÝNEM)

After the St Vitus Cathedral, the Týn Church is the most important religious building in Prague. Although the three-aisled basilica church is not actually located on Old Town Square, but slightly set back on its east side, behind the Týn Parish School (Týnská škola), it is still the dominant feature on the square, together with the Old Town Hall. Its official name, "Church of Our Lady before Týn", is derived from the Týn Court, to the north-east of the church.

Construction of the church was financed by German merchants. Built in 1365 on the site of an earlier Romanesque and early-gothic structure, the earlier church is documented from 1135; it was part of a hospital for itinerant traders, established in the aforementioned Týn Court. The raw structure of the Týn Church was probably finished by 1385, and from 1390 Peter Parler's cathedral workshop took over the construction management.

TÝN CHURCH (KOSTEL PANNY MARIE PŘED TÝNEM)

Wherever you stand in the lanes of the Old Town, the 80-m-tall (262-ft) twin towers of the Týn Church make for a literally outstanding orientation aid. Seen from the Old Town Square, the right (southern) tower is a little fatter and is popularly known as "Adam", whereas the slimmer tower is gallantly known as "Eve". The high altar is adorned with paintings by Karel Škréta, dating from 1649.

ST NICHOLAS IN THE OLD TOWN (KOSTEL SVATÉHO MIKULÁŠE)

The Church of Saint Nicholas in the north-west corner of the Old Town Square is, just like the church of the same name in the Lesser Town, the work of Kilian Ignaz Dientzenhofer. Born in Prague in 1689, he was the son of an originally Bavarian family of architects. And just like with its counterpart on the left bank of the Vltava, the builders here too attempted to create a stone structure that would symbolize the superiority of Catholicism over all other faiths. Even so, the church, which was dedicated in the year 1737, was secularized only 50 years later and at times used as a warehouse. Later on, military bands performed concerts here, until finally St Nicholas was taken over by the Russian Orthodox community in 1871 and in 1920 was adopted by the Hussite Church. The latter – bearing in mind the architect's original intentions – is not without a degree of irony.

ST NICHOLAS IN THE OLD TOWN (KOSTEL SVATÉHO MIKULÁŠE)

Just how much the architectural design of the church was intended to be visually overwhelming becomes clear when one considers that its giant southern side originally faced what was then only a tiny open square, the poultry market. It was not until the Krennhaus (1901) had been demolished that the views opened out toward Old Town Square. The crystal chandelier inside came from the Russian Orthodox community.

LITTLE SQUARE (MALÉ NÁMEŠTÍ)

South-west of the Old Town Square, Charles Street broadens out rather abruptly into a triangular space, the Little Square. Strollers arriving here from Charles Street generally perceive this intimate space as an overture to the much larger adjacent Old Town Square – those arriving from the opposite direction should keep an eye on the detail. The Little Square, although it may not offer quite as much drama as its bigger brother, certainly presents a more authentic picture of an Old Prague square. Its history goes back to the beginnings of the town's history, and today it it still possible to make out the core of the old settlement in the Romanesque and gothic vaults, as well as some of the details on the façades. In the middle of the Little Square stands a golden fountain, featuring a wrought-iron cage (c. 1520), on whose top sits enthroned a gilded Bohemian lion (c. 1650).

One of the loveliest in the square is the House "At the Three White Roses" (below), which has a Romanesque core. It is mostly just called "House Rott", after the ironmonger who commissioned the conversion in 1897. The corner house "To the Minute" (left) separates the Old Town Square from the Little Square. Gothic in its core and later adorned with sgraffito, it has been part of the Old Town Hall since the late 19th century.

CELETNA LANE (CELETNÁ)

Celetná Lane runs in an easterly direction from the Old Town Square to the Powder Tower, forming the boundary from Old to New Town. The picturesque, winding course largely follows an old trading route. The building stock here is often considerably older than one might imagine from the mainly baroque façades. The same is true for the Sixt Palace right at the start of the street, where once Petrarch resided, as the guest of Charles IV. The palace owes its present name to Jan Sixt of Ottersdorf, the Protestant Old Town chancelor, who bought it in 1567 and whose son Jan Theodor was one of the 27 rebels to be condemned to death after the defeat at White Mountain. Although he was pardoned when he was already on the scaffold, Jan Theodor was not willing to convert to Catholicism, but instead emigrated to Dresden in 1627, whereupon his house was confiscated.

Many bakers, too, cared for the physical well-being of the traders who once sold their wares along the lane; at least that is what we can deduct from the lane's name: celetná comes from the word "calta" (English "tents"), the 14th-century name for the local bakers' guild's plaited loaf or puff-pastry cake. The lane has been popular with buskers and street artists since its conversion into a pedestrian zone.

TÝN COURT – UNGELT (TÝNSKY DVŮR – UNGELT)

There was a ducal customs court behind the Týn Church as early as the 11th century where passing merchants paid their customs duties – called "ungelt" (from German "um Geld", about money), before being allowed to sell their goods. In addition, here foreign traders were able to stable their carts, to store their goods safely, and to find board and lodging in the surrounding inns. The Týn Court guaranteed their customs collectors good earnings into the 18th century. Emperor Ferdinand I gifted a property to one of its long-term administrators, Jakob Granovský of Granov, in 1558. In this, the latter was allowed to build his own palace, with the only proviso that he had to employ a servant who would open and close the gates of the Týn Court. Completed two years later, in 1560, the Granovský Palace with its open loggia on the upper floor is today one of the most striking buildings in the court.

The word "Týn" is linguistically related to the English word "town", which itself developed from Old English "tūn", meaning fence, garden, court, hamlet or village. Here it describes a (customs) yard that is enclosed by a wall or buildings, and which was used as intermediate storage, market and municipal customs office until 1773. Its original plan is preserved, and nearly all the buildings have been renovated.

POWDER TOWER (PRAŠNÁ BRÁNA)

Initially, the 65-m-tall (213-ft) late-gothic Powder Tower was built exclusively as a showpiece. At the time of its construction the New Town had already been built more than 100 years previously – and since its walls were now protecting the terrain of Prague, the Old Town fortifications (including also a precursor of the Powder Tower) had lost their original function. The Old Town magistrate asked Vladislav II, whose royal court was in the immediate vicinity, to lay the foundation stone in 1475. After Matěj Rejsek took over the construction management in 1478, the tower was built up to the upper gallery. In 1484, when King Vladislav II moved his residence back to Prague Castle, work on the tower was stopped. Later, a temporary roof was added, and during the 18th century, gun powder was stored in the tower – which explains its name.

During the 13th century, a fortified gate stood in the place of the Powder Tower: "Gothic Prague, Renaissance Prague, the Prague of the 19th century – what is important is the character. The strange, at times sinister, lanes are of a rather grandiose romanticism ... What words are there to describe how splendid an evening is on the river, or how mellow the light is in the Old Town ...?" (Julien Green).

AGNES CONVENT (ANEŽSKÝ KLÁŠTER)

In about 1234, Princess Agnes, the youngest daughter of King Ottokar I Přemysl (c. 1155–1230) and the sister of his successor King Wenceslas I (c. 1205–1255), succeeded in persuading her brother to found a convent of the Poor Clares (modeled on the one founded by the order of Saint Clare of Assisi). She herself also preferred life in the convent to that in a planned marriage, and she dedicated her life to her faith and care of the poor – as abbess from 1235 to 1237. Enlarged by a Franciscan Minorite monastery in 1240, the complex encompasses important religious buildings, such as the churches of St Barbara (1250 to 1280) and St Francis (c. 1250), built in the style of the Burgundian Cistercian Gothic, St Savior (1275–1280) is considered the most important example of the early Bohemian gothic style. During its restoration, the tomb of St Agnes was discovered at the convent.

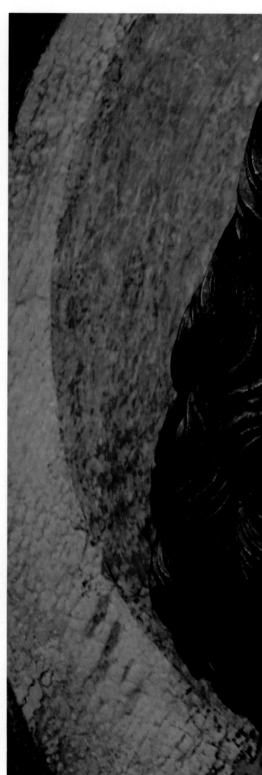

Left, in the foreground of the picture, is the Church of St Savior, behind it the choir of the Church of St Francis. Below left a chapel dedicated to the Virgin Mary. Also worth visiting in the convent is an exhibition of medieval art owned by the National Gallery (below and center, a wooden statue of St Ulrich of Zell created in around 1380/1390 and the carved head of John the Baptist dating from 1509).

A WOMAN'S FATE IN THE MIDDLE AGES: SAINT AGNES OF BOHEMIA

If it is said about a woman that she had rejected all marriage proposals and instead chosen the "crown of virginity", one has to assume that we are dealing with a saint. In this particular case, though, canonization took a long while to come – some 700 years to be precise. For this is how long it took before Pope John Paul II made Agnes of Bohemia (Anežka Česká, 1211–1281) a saint on November 12, 1989. The daughter of King Ottokar I Přemysl and his second wife Constance of Hungary and born in Prague, Agnes was engaged to be married to her cousin Boleslaw of Silesia when she was only three years old. The girl was handed over to her future mother-in-law to be educated. When Boleslaw died, her father promised the then-eight-year-old to the nine-year-old son of the German emperor, the future King Henry IV, who eventually however married someone else. When she had finally grown up, Agnes no longer wished to be married at all, not even to Frederick II who asked for her hand in marriage – and who could blame her? Agnes was not able to lead an independent life until after her father's death. With the support of her brother, King Wenceslas I, she founded a hospital for the poor in 1232, administered by the Franciscans. Then she established a Convent of the Poor Clares, which she herself joined in 1234.

A WOMAN'S FATE IN THE MIDDLE AGES: SAINT AGNES OF BOHEMIA

Agnes preferred spiritual reflection, a life with God, to the dynastic thinking of her day.
Left: In this triptych inside the church, dating from 1350, Saint Agnes (on the right in the picture) can be seen next to St Clare of Assisi, who founded the Order of the Poor Clares. The two saints are believed to have exchanged letters. Below: the National Gallery's exhibition in the St Agnes Convent.

MUNICIPAL HOUSE (OBECNÍ DŮM)

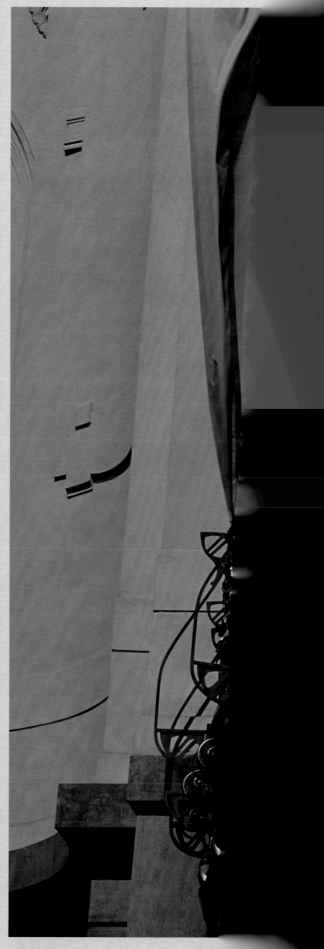

MUNICIPAL HOUSE (OBECNÍ DŮM)

The Municipal House, built in the years 1905 to 1911 according to the plans of Osvald Polívka and Antonín Balšánek, creates a charming contrast to the medieval Powder Tower located to its south-west. Also known as Representative House (Reprezentačni dům) and abbreviated as "Repre" by Praguers, it was built on the site of the royal court founded in 1380. For security reasons, the latter was abandoned in 1483 in favor of a residence on the Hradčany Hill. A fire in the 17th century severely damaged the building; it was rebuilt afterward, however, and a cadet school was housed here. The Municipal House was to be a new prestigious building, laid out on an irregular rhomboid plan, so demanded the municipal government – a major challenge for the architects. They mastered it beautifully, though, creating one of the most attractive Art Nouveau buildings in Prague.

MUNICIPAL HOUSE (OBECNÍ DŮM)

The mosaic on the pediment (left) was created by Karel Špillar as a "homage to Prague"; Alphonse Mucha was responsible for the decor and ceiling fresco in the mayor's office (below left and below right, picture 2). Also noteworthy are the glass mosaics of the main entrance (below right, top). Below right, bottom: the Art Nouveau Café Kavárna Obecní Dům; below right picture 3, a view of the building's lobby.

MUNICIPAL HOUSE (OBECNÍ DŮM)

Right from the start, the Municipal House was designed to offer room for both the public administration services as well as cultural events – such as the Smetana Hall, one of the city's most important concert halls. However, the structure and design of the two-floor building with its huge, rectangular windows and banded rustication at street level, the large balcony, the giant, round-arched windows on the second floor, flanked by decorative pilasters, and the roof, adorned with Art Nouveau motifs, were all intended to give the impression that this is in no ways a multi-purpose hall but rather a "temple of the arts". The Philharmonic Orchestra (founded in 1894), which includes musicians from the National Theater and ranks as one of the ten best orchestras in Europe, often guests in the Smetana Hall.

MUNICIPAL HOUSE (OBECNÍ DŮM)

The Smetana Hall is reached via a wide, sweeping staircase. The interior accommodates 1,500 spectators, with light streaming into the auditorium via the domed glass roof. The platform is flanked by two groups of allegorical statues by Ladislav Šaloun, featuring the Vyšehrad and Slav dances. The murals and ceiling frescoes by Karel Špillar show allegories of the arts – music, dance, poetry and drama.

ALPHONSE MARIA MUCHA: "I DID IT MY WAY"

Of all the artists involved with the embellishment of the Municipal House, Alphonse Maria Mucha (1868–1939) was the most controversial. His colleagues accused him, saying his successes had gone to his head and reproached him for preferring to work alone. In fact, a degree of self-confidence has never been to the disadvantage of an artist. As regards Mucha, he was easily able to shoulder the accusation that he had dedicated his talent not to his home town alone, as Prague was not in fact his home town. Born in the southern Moravian town of Ivančice, Mucha initially worked as a painter of theatrical sets in Vienna, before studying art in Munich and Paris. He had his great breakthrough in the city on the Seine virtually overnight in 1894, when he designed a poster for the actress Sarah Bernhardt. It so delighted "la divina" ("the Divine") that she employed him on contract for six years. After that, Mucha made waves with his work for the Paris World Exposition in 1900. He taught art in New York, Philadelphia and Chicago, returning to his fatherland in 1910 in order to work on his "Slav Epic", a series of twenty monumental paintings. Mucha died in Prague and was buried on the Vyšehrad. During his life, the artist knew how to describe his art in simple yet irrefutable terms: "I did it my way."

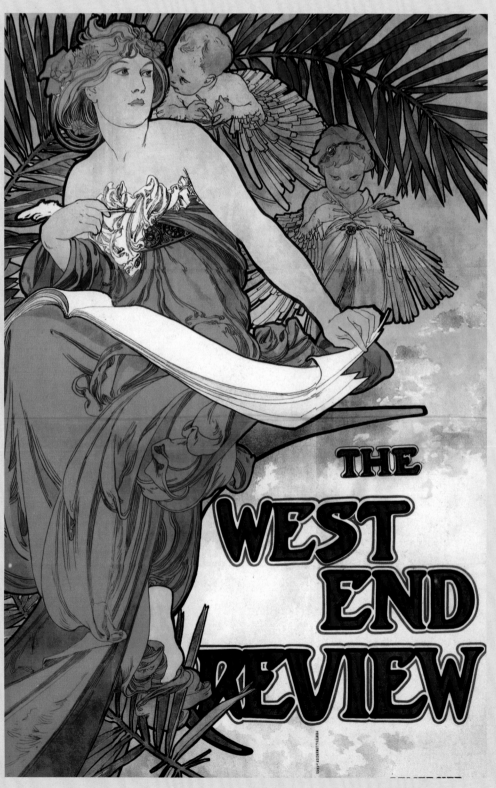

ALPHONSE MARIA MUCHA: "I DID IT MY WAY"

At the turn from the 19th to the 20th century, Mucha (below left, a photograph of the artist taken in about 1900; next to this, some of his poster designs; left, the stained-glass windows he created in 1931 for the St Vitus Cathedral) had already left his mark on both art and crafts to such a degree that many spoke of the "Mucha Style" instead of "Art Nouveau" or "Secession". His posters are still being reprinted today.

PARIS STREET (PAŘÍŽSKÁ)

If after a visit to the Agnes Convent, after reflection and divine temptation, visitors look forward to some earthly pleasures, a stroll along this luxury shopping street will provide the starkest contrast. Paris Street – and it is no coincidence that it was named after the metropolis on the Seine – was laid out on the occasion of the redevelopment of the former Jewish ghetto at the end of the 19th century. It runs from Old Town Square in a north-westerly direction to the banks of the Vltava. Here the Čech Bridge (Čechův most), built in the years 1905 to 1908 in the Art Nouveau style to the plans of the architect Jan Koula, and measuring just under 170 m (558 ft) long and 16 m (52 ft) wide, links Josefov, the Jewish Quarter, with the quay of the Letná Park opposite. Paris Street is lined on both sides by buildings that were designed in a particularly pure and elegant neobaroque or Art Nouveau style.

PARIS STREET (PAŘÍŽSKÁ)

Today visitors will see many luxurious shops on Paris Street, a street modeled on Haussmann's grands boulevards in Paris. However, Franz Kafka felt that the "unhealthy old Jewish town within us is far more real than the new hygienic town around us"; the "hidden corners, the secret passages, the blind windows, the dirty backyards, the ... gloomy taverns all live on inside us".

THE PRAGUE GHETTO

A Jewish community is Prague is documented as early as the 10th century, making it one of the oldest and most important in the Western world. From the 13th century, Jews lived in their own city district, all around the Old New Synagogue. The district became a ghetto when a papal decree determined that Jews should only be allowed to live inside a walled area – well separated from the Christians. Today only little remains of the narrow lanes and medieval houses in the labyrinthine district: the former Jewish Town Hall, six synagogues and part of the Old Jewish Cemetery. Everything else was demolished at the beginning of the 20th century, in order to make room for modern Prague. Memories of the Prague Ghetto, beset several times in its history by fires and the plague, as well as terrible pogroms, are kept alive by the present Jewish community, which counts some 1,600 members. They also run the Jewish Museum, founded in the Old Town in 1906 by the Hebraist Salomon Hugo Liebern. One of the oldest Jewish museums in the world, its exhibitions are laid out in an impressive tour of six historic sites within the former Jewish town: Maisel Synagogue, Klausen Synagogue, Pinkas Synagogue and Spanish Synagogue, Old Jewish Cemetery and Jewish Ceremonial Hall.

The Spanish Synagogue (Španělská synagoga; all pictures) stands on the site of the city's first synagogue, founded in the 12th century, the "Old School" ("Stará škola"). During the 15th and 16th centuries, it became a center for the Sephardi Jews that had been expelled from Spain in 1492. The new building, completed in 1893 to the plans of Ignaz Ullmann, was built in the Moorish (Mudéjar) style in their honor.

OLD NEW SYNAGOGUE (STARONOVÁ SYNAGÓGA)

This synagogue, built as Prague's second Jewish place of worship in about 1270, is the oldest preserved synagogue in Europe where religious services are still held today. It is also one of the earliest gothic buildings in the city, featuring stylistic similarities with the early Cistercian Gothic. It was built by the royal building lodge, which was at that time also still occupied with the construction of the Agnes Convent, and probably intended to accommodate the influx of German Jews from Regensburg, Speyer and Worms. The synagogue's best-known rabbi was the scholar Jehuda Liwa ben Bezalel, known as "Rabbi Loew" (1512–1609), the legendary creator of the "Golem". The Golem (Hebrew for "lump") was a mythical, human-like figure, formed from clay and brought to life for a while by magical powers. Its remains are, so it is said, still hidden in the synagogue's loft today.

OLD NEW SYNAGOGUE (STARONOVÁ SYNAGÓGA)

It is not known how the name of the synagogue (below the prayer room; left the western façade with the former Jewish Town Hall on the right in the picture) came about. Possibly it is a derivation of the Hebrew word "altnai" ("temporary", "under the condition that"), which might refer to a legend according to which the angels "borrowed" the stones for building the synagogue from the Temple in Jerusalem (until the Last Judgement).

THE EMPEROR AND HIS BANKER

"The Jews say of him that when the entire city has a black year, his has been boiled in milk" (Leo Perutz). The reference is to Mordechai (Markus) Maisel (1528–1601), court banker and primate of the Jewish Quarter under Emperor Rudolf II, one of the wealthiest men of his day. An important financier, he was able to obtain some concessions from the emperor, which made life easier for the Jews in Prague. However, it was not altruism that moved the emperor to make those concessions, rather he saw them offset in a countertrade: in return, Maisel had to make half his wealth over to him. However, since the fate of the Prague Jews seems to have been closer to Maisel's heart than the imperial portfolio, he found a way to make his legacy at the end of his days comparatively modest: Maisel entered the annals of the city's history as one of its most important commissioners of build-ing work and a major patron of the arts. Among other projects, he donated to the Jewish community a poorhouse and a hospital as well as several Talmud schools. He also financed the Klausen Synagogue, built toward the end of the 16th century immediately adjacent to the Old Jewish Cemetery. From 1592, he had the Maisel Synagogue, named after him, built for himself and his family. The Jewish Town Hall, too, was donated by Maisel.

Mordechai Maisel is one of the central characters in Leo Perutz's novel "By Night under the Stone Bridge", in which the author brings the Prague of Rudolf II back to life. Today, the Jewish Museum presents two permanent exhibitions in "his" synagogues: the history of Jews in Bohemia and Moravia is detailed in the Maisel Synagogue (left) and Jewish traditions and customs are explained in the Klausen Synagogue (below).

OLD JEWISH CEMETERY (STARÝ ŽIDOVSKÝ HŘBITOV)

"All the legends and songs that came to birth in that city are filled with longing for a prophesied day when the city would be destroyed by five successive blows from a gigantic fist. It is also for this reason that the city has a closed fist in its coat of arms" (Franz Kafka). The oldest tombstone on the Old Cemetery, which was laid out in the first half of the 15th century, dates from 1439 and belongs to the scholar and poet Avigdor Kara. The last funeral took place here in 1787, and even before then a new cemetery, the second oldest Jewish Cemetery, was established in the Žižkov district. It was built because the city was hit by the plague in 1680, and at that time it was forbidden to bury plague victims in the other cemetery. Kafka, too, who died on June 3, 1924, was buried at Žižkov, but his tomb can be found in a more recent Jewish cemetery, which was founded as late as in 1890.

OLD JEWISH CEMETERY (STARÝ ŽIDOVSKÝ HŘBITOV)

The most famous grave in the Old Jewish Cemetery is that of Rabbi Loew (below right, picture 2). There are nearly 12,000 tombstones in the cemetery, although the number of dead buried here is likely to have been much higher. According to Jewish law, graves exist eternally, so when the cemetery, enlarged several times, became too small, earth was heaped up so that new graves could sit on top of older ones.

PINKAS SYNAGOGUE (PINKASOVA SYNAGOGA)

The building history of the Pinkas Synagogue goes back to the early Middle Ages – and a Talmud school can be traced back as early as the 11th century. The synagogue is named after the Rabbi Pinkas, who sold his house to the Horowitz Family in the 14th century. Aaron Meshullam Horowitz had the Pinkas Synagogue built between this building and the south side of the Old Jewish Cemetery in 1535. In the years after World War II, the synagogue was con-verted into a memorial for the Czech and Moravian Jews who were murdered by the National Socialist regime. On the upper floor of the synagogue, an exhibition presents the drawings made by children at the Theresienstadt concentration camp. The pictures date from the year 1942 to 1944, when more than 10,000 children under the age of 15 years were incarcerated there and suffered a cruel fate in the camp or were deported.

PINKAS SYNAGOGUE (PINKASOVA SYNAGOGA)

The names of around 80,000 Czech and Moravian Jews who were killed by the National Socialists are listed on the walls of the synagogue, together with their birth and death dates and the names of their home communes. In 1968, the synagogue had to be closed as it was in danger of being flooded by groundwater. The necessary repairs – deliberately delayed by the communist government – were not completed until 1990.

RUDOLFINUM (RUDOLFINUM)

The architect of the Museum of Decorative Arts, Josef Schulz, was also involved, together with Josef Zítek, in the construction of the nearby Rudolfinum, the present headquarters of the Czech Philharmonic. The "House of Artists" (Dům umělců) was built around 1880 and named after its patron, the Austrian Crown-Prince Rudolf. Originally intended as a concert hall and exhibition space, the Czech parliament sat here between the two world wars. During World War II, the Rudolfinum served as headquarters for the German occupiers. A famous "error" happened during this time – the Czech workers "accidentally" dismantled not, as had been demanded by the occupiers, the statue of the Jewish composer Felix Mendelssohn Bartholdy, but instead that of Hitler's favorite composer, Richard Wagner, who had once been involved in antisemitic propaganda against a colleague.

"It is entirely satisfying to spend time waiting before a concert at the top of the grand staircase in the Rudolfinum, one's back leaning into the gentle roar of the illuminated halls, one's gaze directed toward the opposite side of the square and the trams ..." (Petr Král). The Dvořák Hall (below left) is one of the main venues for the annual "Prague Spring" music festival.

MUSEUM OF DECORATIVE ARTS (UMĚLECKOPRŮMYSLOVÉ MUZEUM)

Adjoining the west side of the Old Jewish Cemetery, the Museum of Decorative Arts was founded as early as 1885, but initially presented its collections in the rooms of the Rudolfinum. A separate exhibition building was not constructed until the years from 1897 to 1899, to the plans of the architect and designer Josef Schulz (1814–1917), who was a native of Prague and was influenced by the style of the French neo-Renaissance. Festively opened in 1900, the museum today holds a world-famous collection of glass, ceramics and porcelain as well as furniture (16th–19th centuries) and gold jewelry (15th–19th centuries). Also exhibited at the museum are textiles, graphic and architectural designs as well as photographs dating from the years 1839 to 1950. The museum's important specialist library, which is open to the general public, also holds a collection of 15th-century parchments.

MUSEUM OF DECORATIVE ARTS (UMĚLECKOPRŮMYSLOVÉ MUZEUM)

The façade of the museum, embellished with reliefs symbolizing various crafts and trades, was created by Bohuslav Schnirch and Antonín Popp. The Street of the 17th November ("ulice 17. Litopadu"), where the museum stands, recalls a demonstration in 1939 of Czech students against the National Socialists. The glass windows were designed by the architect (below right; below left the staircase; left goldsmith work).

PRAGUE'S CUBIST ARCHITECTURE

"The function of architecture is twofold", said Jan Kotěra, the father of modern Czech architecture, "first, the constructive creation of space, second ornamentation. The former constitutes the actual truth of architecture; the latter can at best be an expression of that truth." This concept of architecture as the creation of a total and unified work of art implies that the artistic spirit of invention also reveals itself in the attention given to the design of colors and shapes and the selection of the materials to be used. This is particularly true for that current within the movement, which transferred the ideas of Cubism from the world of fine art to that of architecture, and not contenting itself solely with exterior shapes but also applying its ideas to interior design, right down to the design of furniture and items of everyday use. Although this movement prevailed only for a brief period of time, approximately from 1909 to 1925, it still carried within itself the first shoots of modern postwar architecture. The movement is recalled by the Czech Cubism Museum, a part of the National Gallery and based at the "House of the Black Madonna". Visitors to the museum will find the building itself to be an excellent example of Cubist architecture in Prague – conceived as a cube with sharp edges, and providing a calculated amount of space for the play of light and shade.

PRAGUE'S CUBIST ARCHITECTURE

The statue of the Madonna (below left), after whom the "House of the Black Madonna" is named (Celetná 34, all pictures), could easily confuse: it dates back to an earlier baroque structure, whereas the present building is one of the most attractive examples of Cubist architecture in Prague. The museum was designed in 1911–12 by Josef Gočár, who is commemorated by a bust in the building (below right).

NEW TOWN (NOVÉ MĚSTO)

The "New Town" is "new" only when compared with the Old Town, which it adjoins in the south. The impetus in 1348 for the area's development came from Charles IV, under whose auspices Prague rose to become a cultural and economic center second to none in Europe. The New Town expanded quickly and was soon the most densely populated district. Whereas the Old Town was firmly in the hands of wealthy citizens and merchants, as well as a few noblemen, the newly developed quarter was largely populated by craftspeople, day laborers and, from the early 1800s, also by many industrial workers.

Art Nouveau in the central station: "We want and therefore command that the town to be built is to be named New Town ... We grant ... to this new town all the freedoms ... and dignities which the Old Town enjoys and rejoices in" (Charles IV in his foundation charter of the New Town, 1348).

A NEW ART MOVEMENT: YOUNG AND MODERN

Triggered by the euphoric sense of new beginnings at the turn from the 19th to the 20th century, a new art movement had developed from the late 1880s, which became known under various names: in English-speaking countries it is known under the French term "Art Nouveau" (the shop name of a Parisian art dealer), or sometimes as "Modern Style"; in Germany it is called "Jugendstil" (after the magazine "Jugend", founded in 1896); in Austria it is "Secessionsstil" (because a group of young artists separated or seceded from the older, academic tradition); and in Spain it is known as "stile moderniste". The movement was united in its search for the "new whole", a stylistically homogeneous synthesis of the arts, encompassing all areas of artistic creativity. With this movement, its members wanted to deliberately distance themselves from the preceding historicism which had depleted itself in the repetition of traditional forms, and also from the purely mechanistic philosophy of the industrial revolution. The latter led to a drive "back to nature", to the use of organic, often plant-like, smooth shapes. Art Nouveau prevailed only from 1906 to 1914. There was a smooth transition to subsequent art movements – Expressionism and Art Deco – but Art Nouveau continued to exert its influence over both for a long time.

A NEW ART MOVEMENT: YOUNG AND MODERN

Many young Czech architects of the day visited the studio of the Austrian Otto Wagner – and so the Viennese Secession was strongly echoed by the Prague Secession. This is easy to see in the Koruna Palace (below left and right), corner of Wenceslas Square / Na Přkopě Street, built between 1911 and 1914 by Antonín Pfeiffer and Matěj Blecha. Several palaces on Old Town Square (left) also feature Art Nouveau elements.

CENTRAL STATION (HLAVNÍ NÁDRAŽÍ)

One of the most famous examples of the Prague Secession is the Main Railway Station, from where the first trains to Vienna departed in 1871. The original station hall – a neo-Renaissance structure named after Emperor Franz Joseph I – was replaced by the present Art Nouveau building in the first decade of the 20th century, to the plans of Josef Fanta. The main building has two galleries, each featuring a pavilion at the end. The design of the main façade is somewhat unusual, with two towers linked by an arcade, which is reminiscent of medieval stepped gables. The station is decorated with paintings and artistic windows. The sculptural decoration of the façade was the work of Ladislav Šaloun, who also created the Jan Hus memorial on Wenceslas Square. The station was modernized in the 1970s and linked into the metro network, and again completely refurbished in 2011.

CENTRAL STATION (HLAVNÍ NÁDRAŽÍ)

The sense of space inside the station hall reminds one of the Pantheon in Rome – it is as if Charles IV's ambition to create a new Rome in Prague had been implemented here, albeit much later. The vaulted interior is adorned by the mosaic figures of two women, the inscription "Praga mater urbium" (Prague as the "Mother of Cities") and the date of the Czechoslovak independence – October 28, 1918.

JUBILEE SYNAGOGUE (JUBILEJNÍ SYNAGOGA)

Signs of Jewish life can be found everywhere in Prague, including outside the historic heart of the city. Jews have lived in Prague's New Town since its foundation in 1348, when Charles IV allowed them to settle there as long as they "would build in stone and properly". The latter can certainly be said about the youngest and largest synagogue of the Jewish community in Prague, completed in 1906 and intended as a replacement for the Jewish places of worship that had been demolished during the redevelopment of the Jewish Quarter at the end of the 19th century. Accommodating 850 faithful, the synagogue was built in the Mudéjar style, according to the plans of the Viennese architect Wilhelm Stiassny. In the spirit of the time, however, Art Nouveau elements were also incorporated in the Jubilee Synagogue, built for Franz Joseph I's golden jubilee, after which it was named.

JUBILEE SYNAGOGUE (JUBILEJNÍ SYNAGOGA)

Jerusalem Street leads directly from the Main Railway Station to the Jubilee Synagogue (Jeruzalémská 7). Aside from the Old New Synagogue, it is today the only synagogue where the Jewish community still celebrates its services. All others were either demolished or are now used for different purposes. No other synagogue in the world boasts a similar interior decorated with painted Art Nouveau ornaments.

WENCESLAS SQUARE (VÁCLAVSKÉ NÁMĚSTÍ)

When the New Town was founded – covering a far larger area than the Old Town –, three large squares were laid out where markets and parades could take place: the Haymarket (Senovážne náměsti), the Cattle Market (today's Charles Square) and the Horse Market. The latter was renamed "Wenceslas Square" after St Wenceslas of Bohemia in 1848. During the Prague Spring in 1968, many mass rallies and demonstrations took place here against the arrival of troops from the Warsaw Pact, which had come to Czechoslovakia, as it was then, in order to suppress the government's agenda for reform and liberalization. In protest against the Soviet invasion, two students, Jan Palach and Jan Zajíc, set fire to themselves in 1969, not far from the Wenceslas Monument. The square also entered the annals of the city's history in November 1989, as a focal point for the "Velvet Revolution".

WENCESLAS SQUARE (VÁCLAVSKÉ NÁMĚSTÍ)

Thanks to its enormous size – 750 m (2,461 ft) long and 60 m (197 ft) wide – Wenceslas Square resembles a large boulevard rather than a square. The equestrian statue of St Wenceslas, surrounded by Bohemia's four patron saints (Ludmíla, Prokop, Adalbert, Agnes), was created by Josef Václav Myslbeck and erected in 1912. An inscription on the base implores the saints: "Do not let perish us nor our descendants."

HOTEL EUROPA (HOTEL EVROPA)

Built in the years 1903 to 1905, the Hotel Europa is the joint work of architects Bedřich Bendelmayer and Alois Drýak. Considered the gem of the Prague Secession style, the entire range of typical shapes, combining floral and geometric elements, can be found on the exterior façade as well as inside the hotel: decorated balconies, mosaics and gilding abound. As a hotel, the building on Wenceslas Square has long since faded – however, it is well worth visiting the Art Nouveau café on the ground floor, which still largely features its original furnishings. Other than that, the hotel lives on its past glories. In 1912, when it was still known as the the Archduke Stephan Hotel, Franz Kafka read from his recently penned novella, "The Judgment", in the hotel's Hall of Mirrors, exerting "[...] a quiet, desperate magic" (Rudolf Fuchs). It was to be Kafka's first and only public reading.

The house only received its designation as "Grand Hotel Europa", displayed in golden letters on the pediment, after the communist takeover in February 1948. The roof is adorned with a group of statues by Ladislav Šaloun – a lantern surrounded by fairies that lights up at night. Inside the hotel, too, the beautiful features of the Prague Secession can be found in the corridors and saloons, but especially in the café.

LUCERNA PALACE (PALÁC LUCERNA)

The Lucerna Palace, a seven-floor multi-purpose structure built in the years 1907 to 1921 on the west side of Wenceslas Square, houses numerous offices and luxury apartments as well as elegant shopping malls, restaurants and leisure facilities. The latter include an Art Nouveau cinema, which opened as the first of its kind on Wenceslas Square as early as 1909 and seats 820 spectators. The palace also has a ballroom, which at the time was the largest hall in the country. Glittering balls took place here and renowned musicians performed in concert, but it was also the venue for boxing matches. The palace's architect and master of the works was Václav Havel's grandfather. The passageways linking Vodickova and Stepanská Streets and Wenceslas Square created a large complex, covering around 21,000 sq m (225,960 sq ft) – its symbol is a lantern (Latin "lucerna"), hence the name.

LUCERNA PALACE (PALÁC LUCERNA)

In front of the cinema (left) in the Lucerna Palace, a sculpture by the enfant terrible of the Prague art scene, David Černý, causes a stir (below). A parody of the equestrian statue on Wenceslas Square, it shows the saint riding on the belly of an upside-down horse. Černý, who was born in Prague, also proves elsewhere in the city that art is capable of turning things on its head.

PIVO: THE CZECH NATIONAL DRINK

Although the poet Jan Neruda outlined the disadvantages of beer (Czech "pivo") over wine, writing: "Wine lifts the head, beer makes the legs heavy", beer is still the national drink of the Czechs. Many famous beers originally come from Bohemia, especially the type of beer known as pilsner, which is named after the town of Pilsen. Even Budweiser, often considered "the ultimate American" beer, was originally brewed in the town of Budweis, or České

Budějovice in Czech. The American version today is quite different from the Czech Budvar. Nor would Praguers agree with the notion that beer makes you tired and sluggish, asserting instead that its consumption makes you relax – which can only benefit the free flow of ideas. Jaroslav Hašek, who invented the "Good Soldier Schwejk", used to spend a great part of his day in the Prague pub "U Kalicha" ("At the Chalice"), in order to gather inspiration there

for his stories. It was at the bar, too, that Hašek founded his (parody) "Party of Moderate Progress within the Limits of the Law" in the spring of 1911. "At the Chalice" was but one of Prague's large beer halls; the most famous one today is "U Fleků" ("At the Fleks") in the New Town, a pub and microbrewery, or "pivovar", serving a particularly dark beer. Its uninhibited enjoyment could well bring about proof of Jan Neruda's insights.

PIVO: THE CZECH NATIONAL DRINK

"While drinking my first beer, I make it absolutely clear that I do not enjoy answering all sorts of questions; ... after the second beer, I feel that everything I say is extremely important, and this is why I am shouting ... and trumpeting my sentences out to all and sundry so that ... the entire world would have to hear them". This is how the Czech novelist Bohumil Hrabal describes life inside a typical Czech beer hall ("pivnice").

NATIONAL MUSEUM (NÁRODNÍ MUZEUM)

The present National Museum, built from the year 1885 by Josef Schulz in the style of the neo-Renaissance, dominates the south-east side of Wenceslas Square. The original was founded on April 15, 1818, with an opening proclamation by the Society of Patriotic Friends of the Arts, a group of Bohemian aristocrats under the leadership of the paleontologist Count Kasper Maria von Sternberg. Soon a busy period of collecting began – today the museum possesses more than 13 million exhibits. The main building, on Wenceslas Square and featuring a 70-m-tall (230-ft) dome, holds the natural sciences and history departments of the museum, as well as a library comprising more than 3.6 million volumes. The building's bad state of repair was caused by a bomb in World War II, the bullets of Soviet soldiers during the uprising in 1968 and the construction of the Prague Metro in the 1970s.

The Wenceslas Monument (left; below inside the impressive structure) looks like a protective figurehead in front of the National Museum. At first, the equestrian statue was to adorn the middle of the ramp in front of the building – however, the plan was vetoed by the architect. Since 2011, and probably continuing until 2016, the building is being completely renovated, at an estimated cost of 190 million euros.

PRAGUE COFFEEHOUSE CULTURE: STARBUCKS OR GRAND CAFÉ?

During the 19th century, the coffeehouses of Prague and Vienna were popular meeting places for all those who looked – and found – a second living room there. Kafka's favorite Café Arco today houses the canteen of the police headquarters – but there is now a "Café Franz Kafka" – it has nothing whatsoever to do with the great literary figure, but is merely an attempt to lure in U.S. American tourists, signifying clearly that the great era of Prague coffeehouse culture is over. Whereas there are still some 200 old-style coffeehouses in Vienna, Prague only has just under a dozen, counting generously. In the 1920s and 1930s, the golden city also boasted more than 150 cafés. It was a question of one's intellectual and political views which coffeehouse one would frequent, and when: German Jewish intellectuals met at the "Arco", in the "Continental" or in the Louvre, whereas their Czech contemporaries preferred the "Slavia". One of only a few "bilingual" cafés was the "Central", where Egon Erwin Kisch, the "roving reporter", liked to while away the time. Yet Kisch also loved the "Grand Café Louvre" in National Street, which reopened in 1990, reconnecting with the old traditions. Just as well, because many of the other traditional cafés have long since made room for the paper cups used in the branches of the global Starbucks chain.

PRAGUE COFFEEHOUSE CULTURE: STARBUCKS OR GRAND CAFÉ?

Prague has a coffee museum where visitors can admire old roasting machines. This does not mean, however, that the Prague coffeehouse culture is old and dusty like a museum. Café Slavia (left) is one of only few that survived the period of socialist rule. Café Imperial (below) and the community center (far left) try to bridge the gulf between tradition and modernity.

PRAGUE STATE OPERA (STÁTNÍ OPERA PRAHA)

Competition is good for business – and this is also true for the arts. Thus, the "New German Theater", which opened on January 5, 1888, with the premiere of Wagner's opera "The Master Singers of Nuremberg", is the result of national rivalries, namely between the Czech and German-speaking citizens of Prague. The Czechs had laid a foundation stone for "their own" national theater some 20 years earlier, and so the Germans now needed to build a stage of their own that would be much larger. Indeed, the Prague State Opera is still the largest theater in the city today – yet, ironically, both stages were amalgamated as a single theater in January 2012. Whether this will help to raise the level of artistic quality, however, is doubtful – the critics now hope, nevertheless, that competition will remain intact between the two stages. For it is good for the arts as well as for business.

PRAGUE STATE OPERA (STÁTNÍ OPERA PRAHA)

Erich Kleiber, Gustav Mahler, Richard Strauss and Bruno Walter have all been conductors at this theater, the outside of which is reminiscent of the Vienna State Opera. It experienced a first heyday under director Alexander Zemlinsky, who enriched the operatic life of the city not only with works of Mozart, but also those of persecuted artists like Paul Hindemith, Erich Wolfgang Korngold, Ernst Krenek and Franz Schreker.

NATIONAL AVENUE (NARODNÍ TŘÍDA)

This grand boulevard, laid out in 1781 on top of the city's filled-in defensive moat, marks the boundary between Old and New Town. Following the former medieval city walls in a south-westerly direction from the center, the avenue links the Bridge of Legions with Jungmann's Square. Initially it was simply called "New Avenue" (Nová Aleje), then it was renamed "Ferdinand Avenue" (Ferdinandova třída), in honor of the Austrian emperor. Its present name dates back to the foundation of the Czechoslovak Republic on October 28, 1918. From that day it was still a long way to the events on November 17, 1989, when the brutal crackdown of the students' peaceful demonstration by government forces triggered what became known as the "Velvet Revolution", thus ringing in the end of communist rule.

National Avenue has always been a popular boulevard with the people of Prague, even if many beautiful older buildings had to make way for the transformations and new structures of the 20th century (far left, the glass block of the National Theater's New Stage; left, a modern residential block; below right a new shopping mall). Luckily, the National Theater (below left) was spared the fate of modernization.

NATIONAL THEATER (NÁRODNÍ DIVADLO)

Diagonally across from Slav Island, on the Vltava right bank, stands the National Theater. It was intended as an architectural "riposte" by Prague's Czech-speaking population to the many cultural institutions that were then firmly under German Bohemian or Austrian control. Built by Josef Zítek in the years 1868 to 1881 in the style of the neo-Renaissance, the theater was in the main financed by donations from Czech citizens – which is also documented by the inscription above the entrance, "The Nation Unto Itself". Two months after its completion, this "Golden Chapel on the Vltava" burned down after a major fire; however, restoration work was begun immediately and enthusiastically, and as soon as November 18, 1883, its inauguration was celebrated for a second time – again with Smetana's opera dedicated to the legendary founder mother of the city of Prague, "Libuše".

The foundation stone for this stone manifesto of Czech nationalism was taken from the Říp Mountain. From this peak, the legendary forefather Čech is said to have glimpsed his new fatherland before settling there; it was named Česko after him. As Jan Masaryk, son of the first Czech president commented much later: "The idiot, how could he settle us in a space between the Germans and the Russians?"

SLAV ISLAND (SLOVANSKÝ OSTROV)

Slav Island, which was created by alluvial deposits during the 18th century, was in 1784 surrounded by a ring of dams to protect it from flooding. It owes its present name to the "Pan-Slav Congress", which took place there in the revolutionary year of 1848, and which opposed the policies of assimilation of both Prussia and the Habsburg Empire. Previously the island had been known as "Sophia's Island" ("Žofín ostrov") – in honor of Archduchess Sophie, the mother of Emperor Franz Joseph II. Also named after her is the concert hall, seating an audience of 400, where renowned musicians, such as Liszt and Berlioz, have performed since the 1830s. In the south of the island, the architect Otakar Novotný built the Mánes House – the exhibition hall of an association of artists founded in 1887 and named after the painter Josef Mánes. Their stated aim was to create a stir in the art establishment.

The Šitka Water Tower, immediately adjacent to the Constructivist Mánes House (below; left an exhibition at the Mánes Gallery), was built in the 15th century for the owner of the mill, Jan Šitka. It is one of four water towers which supplied the public fountains as well as the breweries of the New Town. The tower was not crowned with its baroque onion dome until the 18th century.

FILM CITY PRAGUE: THE HOLLYWOOD OF THE EAST

What do Barbra Streisand's "Yentl", Brian de Palma's "Mission: Impossible", Andrew Adamson's "The Chronicles of Narnia" and Martin Campbell's "James Bond 007: Casino Royale" have in common? – All these films were shot in the "Hollywood of the East", yet another epithet for Prague. On the one hand, the city boasts one of the oldest, largest and (according to Roman Polanski even the world's) best film studios, the Barrandow Studios, founded by Václav Havel's family and celebrating their 80-year anniversary in 2011. And on the other hand, the city itself offers a backdrop that is both charming and adaptable like virtually no other. Whether spy thriller or costume drama, whodunnit or biopic, the city on the Vltava is the perfect location for all genres of films. In addition, the production costs here are still some 30 per cent lower than in the West. Nor is there any lack of qualified personnel. Prague's Film and TV School of the Academy of Performing Arts in Prague (FAMU), founded in 1941, enjoys an excellent reputation around the world. Although its most famous graduate, Miloš Forman, left the city when his film "The Fireman's Ball" (1968) was banned, he returned in 1984 with his film "Amadeus", which was awarded eight Oscars. Ever since his resounding success, Prague has become established internationally as "Hollywood of the East".

Whether "Amadeus" or "Mission: Impossible" – Prague rolls out the red carpet for Hollywood stars like Natalie Portman (below left, at the Prague premiere of Miloš Forman's "Goya's Ghosts"), but it also proudly looks back on its own illustrious tradition as a film city. Somewhere in the lanes, a film is always being shot (below right), and the Vltava is a popular subject too (left, "Mission: Impossible – Ghost Protocol").

CHARLES SQUARE (KARLOVO NÁMĚSTÍ)

At 530 m (1,739 ft) long and 150 m (492 ft) wide, Charles Square, originally laid out as a cattle market, is the largest square in Prague. In its middle, Charles IV had the imperial crown jewels exhibited each year in May – initially in a wooden tower, then in the Chapel of Corpus Christi, which was built in 1393 and modeled on the Palatine Chapel in Aachen, Germany, and demolished in 1791. The jewels included relics which were believed to bring miraculous cures and absolution from sins. Worldly affairs, however, were better handled in the New Town Hall, which was built around 1348 in the north-east of the square. Also worth seeing are the Faust House, a baroque and Renaissance palace on the corner of Vyšehradská, where Doctor Faustus supposedly sold his soul, and the Jesuit Church of St Ignatius, completed in 1671, on the east side of Charles Square.

The New Town Hall (all pictures) on Charles Square was the site of the First Defenestration of Prague on July 30, 1419, when the Hussite preacher Jan Zelivský and his followers demanded the release from prison of their fellow believers. Not only were their demands rejected but they were also ridiculed, and so they charged into the offices and threw seven Catholic councillors out of the window.

DANCING HOUSE (TANČICÍ DŮM)

Anyone strolling through the New Town and unexpectedly coming across the so-called "Dancing House" might start to wonder whether they might have had a little too much of the Czech national drink over lunch, perhaps at the "U Fleků". For one part of the glass and steel office complex, which towers here above visitors, appears to stand not only at a slant but also seems to be moving, whereas the other part of the building seems to stand stock still and straight as a candle. Responsible for this impression, which may well irritate at first glance, are the U.S. American architect Frank Gehry and his partner Vlado Milunič, who was born in Zagreb and has resided in Prague for a long time. Like Václav Havel, the latter lived for years in a house next to the vacant spot. Finally, he found a Dutch insurance company willing to invest in the building project, which was completed in 1996.

"Deconstructivist" is how the architect Frank Gehry calls his style; put more simply one could explain it as "modular building" – constructing, taking apart, reassembling. The people of Prague have affectionately named the building, which also houses a gourmet restaurant, "Fred and Ginger"; and indeed the impression of a dancing couple is obvious – she pushes tempestuously while he remains solemnly rigid.

FROM THE NEW WORLD: DVOŘÁK

Born in Nelahozeves near Prague, the son of an innkeeper and butcher, Antonín Dvořák (1841–1904) showed a musical talent early on. When he was sixteen years old, Dvořák went to the capital where he studied at an organ school and worked as a violist in several orchestras (from 1862 to 1871 under Smetana). He was strongly encouraged by Johannes Brahms, who became a lifelong friend. Brahms also advocated that his works, which were initially oriented on the Viennese classics, and then inspired by German composers such as Schumann, Brahms and, to a lesser degree, Wagner, should be published. Dvořák became known to a wider public with his "Moravian Duets" (Opus 32, 1876), "Slavonic Dances" (Opus 46, 1878) and "Slavonic Rhapsodies" (Opus 45, 1878). His most famous work, however, Symphony No. 9, entitled "From the New World" (Opus 95, 1893), combined Bohemian and Moravian folk music with elements of traditional U.S. American music. The symphony was the product of his three-year stay in the United States, as the director of the New York National Conservatory. Dvořák collapsed during the premiere of his opera "Armida" at the Prague National Theater on March 25, 1904, and died only a few weeks later after a stroke, leaving many of his works unfinished.

The Villa America (Letohrádek Amerika), a summer palace built between 1717 and 1720 by Kilian Ignaz Dientzenhofer for Count Michna of Vacínow, today houses the Dvořák Museum. Aside from his piano and viola, visitors can also admire the composer's original scores. The villa's name, by the way, does not refer to Dvořák's "From the New World", but to an inn that once stood nearby.

ENVIRONS

There is so much to see in Prague's inner city that few visitors venture into the outer districts. This is a pity for there are several interesting and easily accessible destinations beyond the city limits. These include the extensive Letná Park with its former exhibition area in the north, as well as Prague's legendary second castle hill, Vyšehrad. Then, once visitors have left the densely populated residential blocks of Prague's suburbs behind in order to travel further out into the soft green hills of Central Bohemia, they will come across mighty castles, glorious palaces and tranquil monasteries.

The vineyards were abandoned at the end of the 18th century and in part replaced by tree-lined avenues; today Vinohrady is one of the most desirable residential districts of Prague.
Below: the Church of the Sacred Heart of Our Lord with its monumental belltower.

LETNÁ PARK (LETENSKÉ SADY)

Of Prague's larger green spaces, the Letná Park is closest to the heart of the city, situated to the northeast of the Hradčany, on a plateau in the hills rising above the left bank of the Vltava. It is partly the park's history which allows one to feel "regally" happy here – after all, it was the site of a coronation (that of Ottokar II, in the year 1261) – and partly the stunning views visitors can enjoy from here, probably the best views of the city, huddling in a bend of the Vltava. David Černý's oversized metronome reminds us of the relentless passage of time. Also worth seeing in the west of the plateau, which was converted into a public park in 1858, is the Pavilion of Hanau (Hanvský pavilon). It was built to the plans of Otto Hieser in the Count of Hanau's ironworks for the Jubilee Exhibition of 1891. In 1898, the city council had the neo-baroque structure moved to the plateau and converted into a restaurant.

LETNÁ PARK (LETENSKÉ SADY)

Letná Park offers respite from the hustle and bustle of the city (below), but it is also a popular venue for major events. Pope John Paul II celebrated a mass here in the open air in 1990, and in 1996, Michael Jackson, the "King of Pop", gave a concert in the park. Perhaps he even used David Černý's metronome (left; far left the Hanau Pavilion), erected in 1991, to set the rhythm?

TRADE FAIR PALACE (VELETRŽNÍ PALÁC)

Today, the National Gallery presents large parts of its collection of European Modernism at the Trade Fair Palace, located north-east of Letná Park. The structure, built in the years 1924 to 1928 to the designs of Oldrich Tyl and Josef Fuchs, and made from concrete, iron and glass, was the largest trade fair building in the world in its day. It became a prototype of functionalist construction, where the building's shape has to adapt to its function. Clear, austere lines and geometric areas determine the design. Decoration, which had often been very lavish in the Neoclassical style period just preceding it, and also in the Secession style, makes room for a tendency toward a new sobriety. Le Corbusier, when visiting this building during his stay in Prague in 1928, enthusiastically declared: "I want to congratulate Prague and its architects on being able to bring such a great work to fruition."

The openness of the building, which is almost completely free of load-bearing walls, is quite impressive. Today it again hosts trade fairs. A central hall, which is open up to the glass roof, is surrounded by free-running corridors that give access to the exhibition rooms (left). Among the treasures of the National Gallery (below) is an exquisite collection of French 19th- and 20th-century art.

ROYAL ENCLOSURE (STROMOVKA), EXHIBITION GROUNDS (VÝSTAVIŠTĚ)

Even farther to the north of Letná Park extends what is probably Prague's most beautiful park. The Royal Enclosure was established in 1270 as a game park for King Ottokar II Přemysl, and goes by the lovely name of "Tree Garden" ("Stromovka"). In the 16th century, during the reign of Rudolf II, a water system with an artificial lake was installed there, fed by water from the Vltava River. In 1804, the park was redesigned as an English Garden, and it has been open to the public ever since. Visitors from the nearby city come to stroll along the royal pathways and visit the neogothic summer residence. Dating back in its origins to the end of the 15th century, the palace was converted to the Tudor style in the years 1804 to 1806, and thus adapted to the idea of an English Garden. In the south-east of the enclosure are the famous exhibition grounds, featuring the Industrial Palace and the Lapidarium.

The Industrial Palace (below) in the Exhibition Grounds, established in 1891 for the Jubilee Exhibition of Bohemian Industry, is an iron and glass structure measuring 238-m-long (781-ft). Its left wing was destroyed by a large fire in 2008. In the same grounds, the National Museum's Lapidarium presents, among other items, in its exhibition rooms some original sculptures from the Charles Bridge (left).

TROJA PALACE (TROJSKÝ ZÁMEK)

During the 17th century, Count Wenceslas Adalbert of Sternberg (c. 1640–1708), a descendant of the wealthiest of the Bohemian-Moravian aristocracy, had a "villa suburbana" built in his vineyard, on the northern limits of the Prague Valley. The summer residence was to be like those he had encountered in Italy. The three-winged palace was designed by Jean Baptiste Mathey – however, the wings were not arranged around a central court of honor after the French model but faced the garden, and as such also the flood plains. The garden, on the other hand is "French", that is, strictly formal in design, its main path leading straight from the Vltava up to the double flight of stairs, completed in 1703. It is decorated with statues designed by the Dresden sculptor Johann Georg Heermann and representing scenes form ancient mythology – the battle of the Olympic gods against the giants.

TROJA PALACE (TROJSKÝ ZÁMEK)

Today, the National Gallery presents at the Troja Palace works by Czech artists of the 19th century. The murals and ceiling frescoes in the Imperial Hall created by the Dutch master Abraham Godin between 1691 and 1697 (below) show the three virtues that the Habsburgs liked to pride themselves for: moderation, clemency and godliness. Left: a fountain in the palace garden, laid out by Jiří Seemann in 1698.

BŘEVNOV MONASTERY (KLÁŠTER BŘEVNOV), STAR SUMMER PALACE (LETOHRÁDEK HVĚZDA)

Břevnov, the first Bohemian friary, was founded in the year 993 by Duke Boleslav II and St Adalbert of Prague (Vojtěch), who was then the city's bishop. Altered many times in subsequent years, the oldest parts of this Benedictine monastery, dating back as far as the 10th century, were only discovered during excavations in 1964. Particularly worth seeing are the Theresian Hall, the monastery's great hall embellished with a fresco by the Bavarian painter and architect Cosmas Damian Asam, as well as St Margaret's Church, built between 1708 and 1714. Around 1556, Archduke Ferdinand of Tyrol commissioned the Star Summer Palace, a hunting lodge, to be built on the slopes of the White Mountain, in the grounds of a game park established there by his father. Today the villa houses an exhibition of the Battle of White Mountain and a Museum of Czech literature.

St Margaret's Church in the Břevnov Monastery (below) was built by Kilian Ignaz Dientzenhofer. The frescoes in the church's nave were created by Johann Jakob Steinfels, the altar images by Peter Brandl. The Star Summer Palace (left) on White Mountain owes its name to the plan on which it was built – a six-sided star. Five of the points are formed by diamond-shaped halls, the sixth holds the stairs to the upper floor.

VINOHRADY

At one time, the royal vineyards ("vinohrady"), for which Charles IV had vines especially imported from Burgundy in the 14th century, were located to the south-east of the inner city, in the district that is still named after them today. There are few sights in the traditional sense to be found here, but it is a lovely place to stroll in the daytime, far from the bustle of the touristic heart of the Golden City, and to pub-crawl at night. There are many small lanes between the main traffic arteries – Vinohradská, Korunní and Francouzská –, lined with second-hand shops, cafés, restaurants, wine bars and pubs. "Rieger's Orchard" ("Riegrovy sady") is a popular beer garden, the largest and most attractive of the green spaces in Vinohrady. The geographic and commercial heart of the district beats on "Peace Square" ("Náměstí Míru"), which is dominated by the neogothic Church of St Ludmila.

The first designs for the brick building of the Church of the Most Sacred Heart of Our Lord were presented by the Slovenian architect Josip Plečnik as early as 1921, but the foundation stone was not laid until 1928. The church was dedicated four years later. It has an unusually monumental bell tower, which occupies almost the entire width of the church above the choir. Its height equals the length of the nave.

SMÍCHOV

This district, adjoining the Lesser Town to the south-east, also once featured slopes planted with vines. Perhaps this was even the reason for naming the area "Laughing Field" ("Smíchov"). The writer Egon Erwin Kisch reports that "during the time of the Rococo" the terrain was "the ultimate in Rococo": "Here the lords of the Bohemian gentry had their summer palaces and gardens, and those who had a particularly privileged mistress, had a *tusculum* built for her in the immediate vicinity ..." (a country house, that is). Yet Kisch does not conceal the fact that the area later became an industrial district – today, Smíchov is booming, and the district has had more glass and concrete built than anywhere else since the end of communist rule. The most spectacular new building is the "Golden Angel" ("Zlatý Anděl"), a glass and steel structure built in 2000 by Jean Nouvel in the heart of the district.

Jean Nouvel's "Golden Angel" (below) formed a clear contrast with the ornate décor of the 19th-century citizens' mansions (left). The name refers to the "House of the Golden Angel" that once stood here. On Nouvel's glass façade, the outlines of an over-life-sized angel can be seen like a shadow – this was the actor Bruno Ganz in Wim Wenders' film "Wings of Desire".

MOZART IN PRAGUE: LOVE AT FIRST SIGHT

"My Praguers understand me." So said the famous composer after the enthusiastic reception his opera "The Marriage of Figaro" received at its premiere in the National Theater in December 1786. It documents the fact that, basically, Wolfgang Amadeus Mozart (1756–1791) had a closer relationship with Prague than with Vienna. The Italian librettist Lorenzo Da Ponte, who wrote the libretti for two more Mozart operas aside from the "Figaro" ("Don Giovanni", 1787, and "Così fan tutte", 1790), was also amazed by the enthusiasm that greeted Mozart's music in the city on the Vltava. He was particularly surprised that, unlike elsewhere, the pieces "were completely understood ... straight away, from the first performance". Mozart in Prague was, so to say, a love at first sight, and this love was certainly not limited only to his music. "Wherever", it is said in a contemporary report, "he went and could be seen, he was greeted with respect and love by the people of Prague who had fallen in love with him." It can safely be assumed that Mozart reciprocated this warmth and affection, and so he dedicated his Symphony No. 38 to the city in 1786, calling it the "Prague Symphony" (KV 504). However, since an artist cannot live on love alone, Mozart frequently returned to his less-beloved but significantly more lucrative Vienna.

MOZART IN PRAGUE: LOVE AT FIRST SIGHT

Five times Mozart visited Prague, three times he stayed at the Villa Bertramka in Smíchov, which by 2009 had been turned into a museum (below left and left; far left, a historic string quartet during a Mozart performance; below right the composer during one of his stays in Prague). There he completed his "Don Giovanni", which was premiered at the Estates Theater that same month, on October 29, 1787.

KINSKÝ VILLA (LETOHRÁD KINSKÝCH)

Like the Dušeks, the musicians who accommodated such illustrious guests as Wolfgang Amadeus Mozart at their Bertramka Villa, the Kinský Family also had a summer home in Smíchov. Count Rudolf Kinský bought the land where once vines had grown in 1825; two years later he commissioned the Viennese architect Heinrich Koch to build an Empire-style villa, which was completed in 1831. In 1901, the estate became the property of the city, which opened the park to the public. One year later, the famous Prague exhibition showcasing works by the French sculptor Auguste Rodin took place here. Today, Villa Kinský is still an inspirational place for the arts – it has housed the ethnographic department of the National Museum, known as "Musaion", since 1922. The Musaion had to be closed in 1986 because of serious structural damage, but in 2005 it was finally reopened to the general public.

The elegant Empire-style villa belonging to the Kinský family is located on a slightly raised part in the lower section of a park, which features a superb stock of old trees (left). The core of the permanent exhibition in the "muses' temple" ("Musaion") is formed by exhibits from around 200,000 items contained in the National Museum's ethnographic collection, one of the most valuable of its kind in Europe (below).

ZBRASLAV CHATEAU (ZÁMEK ZBRASLAV)

Just under 12 km (7.5 miles) to the south of the city, where the Berounka River flows into the Vltava, Knight Zbraslav built a castle – according to legend. Presumably, he had the help of his wife who was endowed with magical abilities; she was the niece of the legendary ancestral mother Libuše, who herself was a visionary. Documentary evidence for a hunting lodge in this idyllic place, built at the same time as the St Jacob's Chapel, exists for the second half of the 13th century, under King Ottokar II. His successor, Wenceslas II, ordered the complex to be converted into a Cistercian monastery in 1292, and this was achieved four years later. Work on the monastery, known as "aula regia" ("Royal Hall"), was completed in 1233. After its dissolution in 1784 under Joseph II, the monastery, which had been given a baroque makeover, was easily converted into a chateau, with only minor alterations.

ZBRASLAV CHATEAU (ZÁMEK ZBRASLAV)

The present appearance of the monastery, which was destroyed during the Hussite wars, dates back to the baroque conversion of the early 18th century, following the plans of Giovanni Santini-Aichl. No longer extant is the old collegiate church, which served as the burial church for the last Přemyslid rulers. The monastery's buildings are arranged in a U-shape, surrounding a court of honor used as cloister.

VYŠEHRAD

"I can see a large city, whose fame will reach the stars, and a place in the woods, about 30 cubits from our Castle (Vyšehrad), and its boundary is formed by the Vltava. When you arrive there you will see a man who carpentered a doorsill in the middle of the wood; and because even the great noblemen must bow low before a sill, you shall give it the name Praha, the 'sill'." Thus the prophecy of Libuše, the youngest daughter of Prince Krok, who after the death of the legendary forefather Čech, led the Czech people who were named after him to Bohemia. And since the prophecy of this visionary daughter seems to have come true, the city of Prague is now located at the foot of not just one, but two castle hills. But then Prague has always been a very special city in every respect...

An Old Slavonic wooden fort, known as the "Upper Castle" ("Vyšehrad"), is said to have stood here as early as the 8th century. A first wooden castle and several churches were built by Prince Vratislav II, who became the first king of Bohemia in April 1085. Only little remains of these; the neogothic Church of Saints Peter and Paul (left) stands on the remains of a Romanesque basilica. The small memorial cemetery (below) dates from 1660.

KARLŠTEJN CASTLE (HRAD KARLŠTEJN)

Karlštejn Castle (Hrad Karlštejn) sits on top of a 320-m-tall (1,050-ft) limestone cliff, in a side valley of the Berounka River, only about 30 km (19 miles) south-west of Prague. It was built between 1348 and 1355 for Charles IV, probably to the plans of the French architect and Prague cathedral master-builder Matthias of Arras. The foundation stone was laid by Arnošt of Pardubice, the first archbishop of Prague, in a festive ceremony. This was rather unusual when a castle was to be built, indicating that Charles IV had his eye on higher things. Organized into three independent complexes, the castle was indeed not intended for military purposes, nor as a palace for the ruler, but was to serve exclusively for the safekeeping of the imperial regalia of the Holy Roman Empire, of the Bohemian crown jewels, as well as of the emperor's own sizeable collection of holy relics.

The most beautiful castle in Bohemia was considered only just good enough as the festive setting for the imperial "treasury". The castle was badly damaged in 1422 during the Hussite attacks and then restored, only to be taken again, this time by the Swedes in 1648. Its present appearance dates back to a neogothic restoration undertaken in the 19th century by Emperor Franz II and his son Ferdinand I.

SACRED CEREMONY: THE "MAGIC WORLD" OF KARLSTEJN CASTLE

he stone-laying ceremony for Karlštejn Castle took lace in the same year as the foundation of Prague's ew Town. And like the ceremonies employed there, hich encompassed both secular and sacred aces, so the outside of Karlštejn Castle, which imbs up the hill as a mirrored L-shape, is also ymbolic of Charles IV's desire to present himself as a eligious ruler. The castle's layout in three steps is in ccordance with medieval concepts of hierarchy: the lowest, "earthly" step, represented by the imperial palace, is followed by the smaller tower with the St Mary's and St Catherine's chapels. The highest, "heavenly" step is symbolized by the big tower of the castle keep, as well as the Chapel of the Holy Cross, reserved for Christ the Redeemer. It was at this highest level that the imperial regalia and the crown jewels were also kept, together with the emperor's relics. The level signified the status the Holy Roman Emperor wished to assign to the worldly symbols which were the symbols of his power, and by that act also to himself. Nor did his religious performance fail to have an impact. "I have just come from Karlštejn", reports the German architect and art historian Sulpiz Boisserée (1783–1854), and declares: "You feel yourself transported into a magical world and see all the bright, golden insanity of your childhood years come true all around you ..."